The Structure and Governance of Public Service Broadcasting

Giorgia Pavani

The Structure and Governance of Public Service Broadcasting

A Comparative Perspective

palgrave
macmillan

Giorgia Pavani
Department of Political and Social Science
Alma Mater Studiorum Università di Bologna
Bologna, Italy

ISBN 978-3-319-96730-1 ISBN 978-3-319-96731-8 (eBook)
https://doi.org/10.1007/978-3-319-96731-8

Library of Congress Control Number: 2018949146

This Palgrave Pivot imprint is published by the registered company Springer Nature Switzerland AG
The registered company address is: Gewerbestrasse 11, 6330 Cham, Switzerland

… though it will never make up for all your dedication
to me over these years,
this book is for you, Luca.
Thank you for helping me to look ahead.

Foreword

Public Service Broadcasting: Models and Governance

Having been part of a school, like that of Paolo Barile in Florence, that was formed on the comparative research method, I feel the importance of presenting this work by Giorgia Pavani on the public service television and its governance.

In the late 1960s, Italy had a solid monopoly governed by limited legislation, through a Convention signed in 1952 and characterized by strict governmental control.

In that period we decided to undertake the study of the different television models adopted in Europe (at least in the major countries), comparing them with the very different ones adopted in North and South America.

Approaching the theme as constitutional lawyers we, therefore, started our analysis by considering Article 21 of the Italian Constitution and the fundamental principles contained therein. Many of the leading scholars in the field, in that period, were studying freedom of expression, rightly considered to be the foundation of the democratic regime, and the increasingly important medium of television was being studied within the context of that freedom.

Before and after Barile, the names of scholars such as Esposito, Elia, Fois, Paladin, Amato and Pace stand out. To some extent all the scholars of the Florentine school addressed these themes, starting from Cheli,

De Siervo, Caretti, Merlini, Grassi and myself. Many of the younger ones continued along this path and of these, I wish to give special mention to Filippo Donati.

The first question that everyone asks themselves, as Giorgia Pavani rightly does, concerns the reasons why radio and television should be regulated. In this case, once again, the answer is provided directly by the Constitution. It is the constitutional system itself, founded on Articles 21 and 41, and initially also on Article 43, that requires a complete and in-depth regulation of this phenomenon.

As in 1948, and from before that in the debates of the Constituent Assembly, the need for a press law was recognized. Over the years, different versions of this were enacted while at the beginning of the 1970s, there was a strong push for a broadcasting law from politicians, legal theorists and then the Constitutional Court itself.

The Constitution, in addition to the obvious freedom of expression and enterprise in the field of information, is based, as the Italian Constitutional Court has pointed out, on the fundamental principle of internal and external pluralism, which implies not only the right to inform but also the right to receive information. It recognizes, in complex editorial structures, the independence of journalists and the editorial independence of the governing bodies of public media companies. Finally, special financing arrangements are guaranteed for the governing bodies of the latter to avoid any form of indirect conditioning.

The first broadcasting law of 1975 is based on these principles, as set out by the Constitutional Court in 1974 (n. 225). This early legislation was followed by further broadcasting laws, in 1993, in 2004 (then transferred into the 2005 Consolidated Text of radio and television) and then in 2015. As we are well aware not all the principles indicated therein have been respected over time, however, these laws progressively built a model of public service that fits within the tradition widespread throughout Europe.

On the other hand, Italy's private broadcasting sector has seen the creation of a model of deregulation, initiated by the famous judgement in 1976 of the Constitutional Court (n. 202); this introduced, consciously or unconsciously, a number of characteristics typical not only of the North American television model, but also many of its contents. The mixed system introduced in those years, which is aptly reflected in the 1990 Mammì law, is a totally original system even on the European scene. The Italian Rai-Mediaset "duopoly" is a subject widely discussed in Europe and not always in positive terms.

Perhaps due to the concern raised by this state of affairs, Europe began to legislate with Directives and Conventions that aimed to create an increasingly uniform European space. The "Television without frontiers" Directive 89/552/EEC, which was accompanied in the Council of Europe by a parallel initiative, i.e. the European Convention on Transfrontier Television (May 5, 1989) clearly has this objective. The "Television without frontiers" Directive, which later became the "Audiovisual Media Services" Directive, is now at its fourth revision. The new version—which will at last include online services that have so far been excluded—should be approved by the end of 2018 and will enter into force in 2019. The current Directive—while recognizing the competence of the Member States in defining the public service—establishes a series of common criteria to be respected in the mixed European radio and television broadcasting system. The TWF Directive sets minimum standards for those wishing to straddle national borders and marks the birth of the European mixed system. It should be noted that Mediaset has battled against this minimum set of rules. This Directive also contains the section on "protected events" that—in common with all free-to-air programmes—establishes common principles on citizens' right to access not only information but also certain events (sports or other) of major importance for society.

In terms of public services, the most significant element of comparison is instead the "Protocol on the system of public broadcasting in the Member States", annexed to the Treaty of Amsterdam (2 October 1997). The introductory note is fundamental in that it directly links the "public broadcasting system" to the "democratic, social and cultural needs of every society, and the need to preserve the pluralism of the media", clearly recalling the constitutional motivations referred to above.

This premise, now common in Europe, clearly strengthens the European model of public services and, of course, their governance.

Giorgia Pavani dedicates her best pages to this topic with an analysis that, in my opinion, will be widely shared. The Italian legislator fluctuated at length, even during the delicate preparatory phases, between reference to the British model of the BBC, especially in the proposals presented by Minister Gentiloni (during the Prodi government) and the French model, structured around the centrality of the Authority. What emerges from the 2015 reform (Law 220) probably does not adhere to either. The model of a governance of public television characterized by an eminent CEO could be positive if the choice were not dependent on an overly strong influence of the majority-Government coupling, which seems to neglect the fundamental precepts of the Court regarding independence.

Such are the early impressions. We hope that, in practice, it will not be so.

Rome, Italy

Roberto Zaccaria
Professor of Public Law,
former Chairman of the RAI

Acknowledgements

The Book and Author wish to thank colleagues Sarah Keating, for her invaluable help in translating and revising many parts of this book, Carlo Ugo de Girolamo for his help in updating the data in Chapter 5 and Sabrina Ragone for her help in reviewing the legal terminology and more besides.

Many thanks also to my editor Lucy Batrouney for assisting me in the preparation of the book and to one of my anonymous reviewers for giving me an idea for developing my research further.

Contents

CHAPTER 1

Introduction

Abstract This chapter introduces the context in which public service broadcasters are analysed today. The changing media landscape impacts not only on the mission of public broadcasters and public service media, but also involves their organizational structure, the composition of their managing bodies and their relationship with the political institutions at a state and regional level, namely their governance. The aim of the book is to examine the various structural and organizational solutions of PSB in Europe, namely the European model, during this transitional period. Particular attention is given to the legal terminology and the dialogue between the social sciences. This study uses the legal methodology to study the structure and governance of PSB taking into account both state and (sometimes) regional legislation, constitutional contexts and supranational regulation that requires compliance with a set of common principles.

Keywords Legal methodology · European models · Public service broadcasters · Public service media · Governance

Context

Writing about public service broadcasting (PSB) today presents a challenge, both as regards content and methodology because it is "a policy project under revision in Europe" (Donders 2012, p. 1).

G. Pavani, *The Structure and Governance of Public Service Broadcasting*, https://doi.org/10.1007/978-3-319-96731-8_1

The transition from the "ancient TV" to the "modern TV"[1] is being carried out through a series of significant policy initiatives enacted by PSB on online platforms (dubbed PSB 2.0: Brevini 2013). It has been noted that "just as the radio was not wiped out by television, so there is no reason to suppose that television will be ousted by the Internet. As each of these tools offers different products, clearly one can be added to another" (Sartori 1997, p. 29).[2] However, in this new scenario, characterized by convergent media forms, the role of the state is in crisis and the existing legislative framework may not always be suitable in light of technological developments. This changing media landscape impacts not only on the mission of public broadcasters but also involves their organizational structure, the composition of their managing bodies and their relationship with the political institutions at a state and regional level, namely their governance.

Many states are engaged in a critical debate over the role of PSB that has generally led to limited reforms; one could almost talk of "legal microsurgery" that regulates no more than the appointment of Board members or the nomination of the President or COE. There has been no attempt at an overall reform of the sector, as illustrated by the cases of Italy, France and Spain (Chapter 6).

At the same time, at a supranational level, the Council of Europe and the European Union have used both soft and hard law to different ends with the goal of strengthening the importance of PSB and to urge states to adopt a regulatory framework that is as far as possible homogeneous and complies with the principles of pluralism and media independence (Donders and Pauwels 2008). This also entails a transparent appointment process for the management bodies (Chapter 3).

As regards the mission and the remits, a prototype PSB that complies with these principles has now risen like a phoenix from the cultural model of the BBC, "sifted" from the ashes by the supranational organizations and based on a series of pan-European standards transposed by national legislatures (Pavani 2016, p. 29).

On the other hand, the structure of the public broadcasters is noticeably heterogeneous, as each state organizes its PSB according to its historical, legal, economic and social traditions. Thus, a broad range of

[1] By contrast with the democracy of Benjamin Constant, the ancient TV is "passive", while the modern TV is "active". See Pavani (2012, p. 12).

[2] Author's translation.

organizational solutions has appeared, often with unique features. The social, political, cultural and legal structure has led to each public broadcaster emerging as an expression of the system to which it belongs, and as far as its organization is concerned, of which it is the result. At the end of the 1960s, Debbasch expressed this concept masterfully: "Les citoyens ont le droit de la radiodiffusion qu'ils méritent" and he urged the jurists to build a "droit de la radio et de la television" (Debbasch 1969, p. 5).

Aim of the Book

The aim of the book is to examine the various structural and organizational solutions of PSB in Europe during this transitional period, in order to:

- illustrate the similarities and differences in the governance of the single national public broadcasters that have evolved within a historical legal model (the European model);
- analyse the determinants of the model by tracing its historical development using a comparative approach and verify its validity in light of the new technological landscape and the homogenizing trends "imposed" at a supranational level;
- highlight the common thread that links recent legislative reforms of governance (or more precisely, of internal organization) of public broadcasters in those European countries that are emblematic of this model (Italy, United Kingdom, Spain, France);
- finally, through a cross-sectional and comparative analysis of legislation, offer a complete picture of the various solutions adopted by states that could constitute a base of useful information for studies in other disciplines (communication sciences, communication sociology and political science, with particular emphasis on public communication, etc.) that will perforce consider the normative framework.

Terminology

In recent years, most public service broadcasters have started to employ the Internet and other digital platforms to relay their services: we are moving from a system of "linear" PSB to a system of new media, so, when referring to media systems, it is often more accurate to employ the term "public service media" (PSM) rather than PSB, as the Council of Europe (CoE) suggests[3] (Psychogiopoulou et al. 2017).

Nonetheless, this study focusses specifically on the public broadcasters, their organizational structure, their governance and the relationship between the political system and their internal organization. The vision that emerges from the study underlines the relevance of the public law approach in the broadcasting sphere, further emphasized by the constitutional context in a number of countries. Hence, when referring to public broadcasters I have chosen to use the term PSB. However, I do use the term PSM—as well as "audiovisual"[4] or "medium/media"—when referring to broadcasting systems in general.

The term PSB includes both radio and television, but it is generally accepted by scholars of the subject that the protagonist in broadcasting is TV (the radio is treated separately only when its regulation differs from that of the TV, as in Barendt 1995, p. 3).

Academic Research

> The field of media communication policy encompasses a variety of theoretical approaches derived from traditional disciplines, such as political science, sociology, economics and law. Hence, each of these fields has contributed to diverse theoretical accounts of how media policies are shaped and developed. (Brevini 2013, p. 19)

Instances of dialogue between the sciences have been rare, however. The same is true for the comparative approach: most of the literature on the media "is highly ethnocentric, in the sense that it refers only to the experience of a single country, yet is written in general terms, as though the model that prevailed in that country were universal" (Hallin and Mancini 2004, p. 2).

This observation is equally valid for legal studies on broadcasting systems, as illustrated by a seminal work that focusses on the study of

[3] Recommendation R (2012) 1 of the Committee of Ministers on public service media governance, note 1.

[4] The origin of the semiotic model of audiovisual—formed from the two words "audio" and "visual"—includes everything that is transmitted/perceived through our sight and hearing (through radio and television, cinema, Internet, etc.) and refers to the communication from many to many. It is, therefore, a more complex term than the object of the present analysis, dedicated to a segment of the audiovisual sector.

the national law of four European states in addition to that of the US (Barendt 1995).

The technical nature of this subject should not discourage jurists from undertaking comparative analyses that also consider the results achieved by other sciences. The new technological landscape invites us to experiment with new approaches of enquiry and push beyond the issues extensively researched by domestic public law studies that generally adopt a top-down approach. Research conducted hitherto has generally been limited to identifying the provider of the television service (public or private) and studying the division of legislative competences between the centre and local government, highlighting the organizational aspects or focussing on the link with freedom of expression, while completely ignoring the political and social context in which the public broadcasters operate.

An analytical approach, aimed at supporting an analysis based on normative texts is insufficient, and may even be misleading when explaining a complex phenomenon like that of PSB: an institution at the service of a fundamental freedom and inherently connected to a country's political environment. We cannot assume that the legal categories used to test the degree of independence of public bodies or subjects and/or independent Authorities can be applied to public broadcasters without adaptation. Any attempt to do so would fail to consider their particular mission and the inevitable two-way relationship with the political system in which they operate (PSB gives voice to political groups and is, at the same time, partly influenced by them).

This context can only be understood if the barriers between the legal sciences and the "other" sciences are overcome and studies on the link between media and politics are not considered as mere decoration for the comparatist inquiry, but rather the key to interpreting certain nuances (and sometimes more besides) in the operation of broadcasting systems. This approach, previously tested with success in public law as well as in private law, makes it possible to highlight some forms of circulation of organizational models of PSB that would be difficult to explain through a positive law analysis alone.

It is, therefore, necessary to draw on data derived from studies in other sciences, such as sociology and the communication studies, and use them as a tool to place the topic under discussion within a legal framework.

The levels of interaction between the sciences, of course, depend on the sensitivity of the comparatist and the object of the research.

Sometimes extrajudicial data can help in understanding the socio-political basis of a specific PSB system (e.g. the Dutch pillarization system). At other times, they can be used to reformulate classifications (as in the case of a decentralized organization, see Chapter 5) or to refute certain procedures (as in the case of the parliamentary appointment of members of management bodies, see Chapter 6).

Methodology

This study uses the legal methodology to study a segment of the European model of PSB—structure and governance—taking into account both state and (sometimes) regional legislation, constitutional contexts and supranational regulation that requires compliance with a set of common principles.

The comparative analysis conducted through "formants" will evidence the creative role of constitutional jurisprudence in outlining the prescriptive characteristics of the model and the cultural reasons that allowed it to circulate outside Europe (Sacco 1991).[5]

The positivistic and normativistic perspective adopted to analyse the organizational structure of public broadcasters will provide some legal data that could constitute a base of useful information for studies in other disciplines that cannot ignore the normative framework (Chapter 5). Some of these data will be interpreted and reviewed while taking into account the classifications and models provided by other sciences. In this way, even if moving from a positivistic and normativistic perspective the "the positive law will not be reduced to the law of the state" and use will be made "of other sciences to analyse the law in force outside the state or states" (Pegoraro 2014, p. 37), and to validate the comparison.

The European model of PSB will be split into its various elements that I consider crucial, each of which can be used to test the degree to which a public broadcaster is actually "public".

[5] As Rodolfo Sacco explains: "even the jurist who seeks a single legal rule, indeed who proceeds from the axiom that there can be only one rule in force, recognizes implicitly that living law contains many different elements such as statutory rules, the formulations of scholars, and the decisions of judges—elements that he keeps separate in his own thinking. [...] we will call them, borrowing from phonetics, the "legal formants" (Sacco 1991, p. 22).

The analysis of positive law will be conducted on the EU member states, as well as two CoE members, Switzerland and Norway, that I have chosen to add to the basket due to certain interesting features they possess (the federal nature of the state, on one hand, and sharing the cultural model of public service that characterizes the Scandinavian countries on the other).

The reference to other non-European countries serves to complete the historical and comparative reconstruction of the two legal models of broadcasting systems. Specifically, the circulation of the US model in Latin America provides an interesting case study to bring out the more public character of televisions in countries labelled—often too hastily—as prototype "commercial TV." Likewise, the strength of the European model can be tested by referring to some countries culturally linked to the United Kingdom. For example, this justifies the focus on Australia, New Zealand and Canada.

Some issues will be addressed by describing individual paradigmatic state experiences (e.g. the decentralization of public broadcasters, the appointments system of the managing bodies); these analyses serve to frame certain determinants of the European model and make it possible to test some current trends.

The thematic approach of the book (not based on single legal systems) makes it possible to expand the book's scope beyond the "big five" that dominate the literature, namely France, Germany, Italy, the United Kingdom and Spain which have been defined as the "trend-setters" in Europe and are the countries generally considered even in the few legal works (Zaccone Teodosi et al. 2008, p. 3).

Structure of the Book

The book is structured as follows:

Chapter 2 will review the justifications, whether economic, cultural, political or technical that led to regulation of the medium of television and the initial choice to subject public TV to the monopolistic system. These justifications will then be applied to the study of the two historical, legal models of regulation (US model and PSB model) and the classifications applied by the scholarship. An analysis will also be provided of the circulation of these around the world.

Chapter 3 identifies the international and European sources regulating the television sector as well as international organizations and the competent European bodies in the sector. The aim is to guide the reader in an understanding of the supranational rules binding the Members (hard law) and those that guide their choices significantly (soft law) and of a number of common principles, shared between the member states of the EU implemented at the state level, in particular, the principle of pluralism and the principle of media independence.

Chapter 4 will consider the constitutional landscape in which PSB has developed. It will enable the reader to place PSB in a specific (constitutional) context and will highlight certain rules that have frequently resulted from judgments in the Constitutional Courts, specifically, the principles of independence and pluralism.

Chapter 5 describes the legal framework of all the selected countries with an analytical-comparative approach and focuses on two important issues to evaluate the independence and pluralism of PSB (decentralized organization of the broadcaster and method of funding).

Chapter 6 analyses data on the structure of PSB in order to pinpoint how the nomination of the managing bodies of public broadcasters actually works and to offer a more realistic analysis of the parliamentary appointments. I will analyse certain emblematic countries (the UK, Italy and Spain).

Chapter 7 contains the conclusions.

References

Barendt, E. (1995). *Broadcasting law: A comparative study.* Oxford: Oxford University Press.

Brevini, B. (2013). *Public service broadcasting online: A comparative European policy study of PSB 2.0.* Basingstoke: Palgrave Macmillan.

Debbasch, C. (1969). *Le droit de la radio et de la télévision.* Paris: PUF.

Donders, K. (2012). *Public service media and policy in Europe.* New York: Palgrave Macmillan.

Donders, K., & Pauwels, C. (2008). Does EU policy challenge the digital future of public service broadcasting? An analysis of the commission's state aid approach to digitization and the public service remit of public broadcasting organizations. *Convergence: The International Journal of Research into New Media Technologies, 14*(3), 295–311.

Hallin, D. C., & Mancini, P. (2004). *Comparing media systems: Three models of media and politics.* New York: Cambridge University Press.

Pavani, G. (2012). *Radiotelevisioni. Profili storici e comparati.* Bologna: Filodiritto Editore.

Pavani, G. (2016). La governance dei sistemi radiotelevisivi pubblici: una questione culturale. *Federalismi.it, Focus Comunicazione, Media e Nuove Tecnologie*, N. 1, 1–33.
Pegoraro, L. (2014). *Diritto costituzionale comparato. La scienza e il metodo*. Bologna: BUP.
Psychogiopoulou, E., Anagnostou, D., Craufurd Smith, R., & Stolte, Y. (2017). The freedom and independence of public service media in Europe: International standards and their domestic implementation. *International Journal of Communication, 11*, 1936–1955.
Sacco, R. (1991). Legal formants: A dynamic approach to comparative law (Installment I of II). *The American Journal of Comparative Law, 39*(1), 1–34.
Sartori, G. (1997). *Homo videns. Televisione e post-pensiero*. Roma-Bari: Laterza.
Zaccone Teodosi, A., Gangemi, G., & Zambardino, B. (2008). *L'occhio del pubblico. Dieci anni di Osservatorio Rai-IslCult sulla televisione europea*. Roma: Rai-Eri.

CHAPTER 2

Models for the Study and Regulation of Broadcasting Systems

Abstract This chapter reviews the justifications, economic, cultural, political and technical that led to regulation of the medium of television and the initial choice to subject public TV to the monopolistic system. These justifications are then applied to the study of the two historical, legal models of regulation (US commercial model and PSB model) and to the classifications applied by the scholarship. An analysis is also provided of the circulation of these two models around the world. The author deals briefly with the origin of PSB in Europe, the cultural features inherited from the BBC model and the circulation of this model outside Europe. Finally, she discusses some (heuristic) cultural models, created by scholars of other social sciences that may help to measure the relationship between the political system and public service broadcasting.

Keywords Regulation · Legal models · Public service broadcasting
US commercial model · PSB models

Introduction

The varying intensity of state regulation of broadcasting (depending on the technical, economic, political and cultural justifications) has led to the formation of two legal models, that of the United States and that of Europe, seen in the literature as being in opposition. Both of these models are influenced by their differing legal traditions and two different

G. Pavani, *The Structure and Governance of Public Service Broadcasting*, https://doi.org/10.1007/978-3-319-96731-8_2

conceptions of public management. These two models no longer exist in their pure form. Except for rare cases of "State TV," broadcasting systems are mixed, with a predominance of either the public or private sector depending on the legal and cultural traditions of the country. The few attempts to classify the structural organization of broadcasting enterprises have failed to withstand the test of time because based on parameters that are no longer relevant such as the forms of state, especially the contrast between states with a socialist ideology and liberal-democratic states. This Chapter will deal briefly with the origin of the two historical legal models of regulation as required for a comparative historical overview, before analyzing their circulation beyond the borders of the United States and Europe.

Why Regulate Television?

By contrast with the press, broadcasting was immediately subjected to extensive regulation and control of both structure and content (Barendt and Hitchens 2000, Ch. 1, §3).[1] The liberal imprint that had characterized the freedom of the press gave way to state interventionism even in countries where the organizational structure of broadcasters is almost entirely determined by the rules of the free market. The reasoning for this approach can be found in certain arguments that today are largely outdated:

- First, the initial electromagnetic spectrum scarcity led states to consider the airwaves as a limited public good (a form of natural monopoly), hence a classic case of market failure justified government intervention (Blumler 1991, p. 7). The debate surrounding this justification involved the Constitution: it was the basis of the famous judgment of the United US Supreme Court *Red Lion Broadcasting Co. v. FCC* and the early judgments on "broadcasting rights" of the German and Italian Constitutional Courts (see Chapter 4). However, from the introduction of cable and satellite broadcasting, any justification related to spectrum scarcity was no longer relevant.

[1] The theme of broadcasting regulation and the reasons that justify/justified State intervention is widely dealt with in the scholarship. Seminal works include: Hoffmann-Riem (1996), Gibbons (1998), and Goldberg et al. (1998, 2009). On the relationhip between TV and the press on the reasons for regulation, see the opposing theses in the classic works: Bollinger (1976, p. 11) and Powe (1987).

- The economic argument depended on the idea of the imperfection of the television market. Closely related to the topic of frequency scarcity was the economic justification based on the greater outlay required by companies when financing a broadcaster than a newspaper (i.e. in the simplest form of implementation of freedom of expression: words written on a sheet of paper). Both reasons have fuelled the opposition between two groups of market failure perspectives: the social democratic perspective that favoured government intervention and those against it, except in the case of real market failure (Hoskins et al. 2004, p. 292).
- The political argument was based on the idea of television as an instrument of political participation and pluralism in democratic societies. The guarantee of the formation of free opinion is a precondition for the exercise of many constitutional liberties and for the democratic functioning of a state. Moreover, for this reason, the regulation of television was considered necessary to remedy the errors of the free market and, in Europe, to reinforce the need for principled public service regulation after the negative experience of the media under Fascism (Humphreys 1996, pp. 116–117). As Sartori recalls, however, "video-politics has an impact on political processes [...] It does not only characterize democracy, the power of the video is also available to dictatorships" (Sartori 1997, pp. 39–40).[2] Many authors see PSB as a tool for ensuring a level of government control over mass media (e.g. Garnham 1990).
- The cultural argument is based on the social function of television. Due to its technical characteristics, since the 1970s, television has been considered a tool that can modify the viewer's perception of transmitted messages and enrich them with emotions and sensibilities that cannot be found in any other medium of communication (Luhmann 2000 and later Tuchman 1980; Baggaley and Duck 1977. "The medium is the message," could sum up the much more complex teaching of Canadian sociologist Herbert Marshall McLuhan). The force of suggestion that television exerts on viewers could lead to it becoming a "bad teacher" that could change the perception of a message and thus it required regulation or some form of "licencing" (Popper and Condry 1994). This rationale was upheld by the

[2] Author's translation.

> US Supreme Court when it cited the example of the perception (and potential danger) of the message for a child audience. Thus, while it is relatively easy to stop a child reading a newspaper, it is more difficult to shield them from exposure to the television message (*FCC v. Pacifica Foundation* 438, US 726, 1978).

Such arguments have justified regulation of the medium of television as well as the initial choice to introduce a monopolistic system within Europe.

The transition from analogue to digital, the phenomenon of convergence and the use of the Internet, have profoundly modified the broadcasting scene. Indeed, the evolution of television in recent years is hardly comparable (in terms of quality and speed of change) to the way it evolved in its first 60/70 years of activity. Such have been the changes that it would be more fitting not to use the singular, i.e. television, but to prefer the plural—discussing as many "televisions" as there are platforms and ways of broadcasting available. TV-web, for example, is an interactive tool comparable to a personal computer that allows the transition from a "from one-to-many" to a "one-to-one" dynamic and from the age of mass communication to an era in which communication is once again interpersonal and interactive because of the constant exchange between the user and the provider.

To consider such phenomena only from the point of view of technological progress would be mistaken and would "lead to a partial understanding of long-term general trends. In the audiovisual sector, [...] new technologies are not invented per se but in response to market demands for greater speed in the circulation of capital, in the productivity of investments and military efficiency" (Lange 2007, pp. 13–14).[3] The idea of applying digital technology to television was, therefore, neither born from individual states nor a response to a demand from users, rather it was a consequence of market needs to which states (and the EU in Europe) were obliged to respond by regulating its effects. This phenomenon intertwines with the cultural phenomenon of globalization and with that of deregulation and has a cascade effect on the economy, on policies of intervention and state regulation, as well as on cultural relations between the states themselves (for a strong criticism of the regulation of the media see Zeno-Zencovich 2008). On the one hand, there is a trend toward

[3] Author's translation.

homogenization in what television offers, despite the increase in usable channels, and a levelling effect between public and private broadcasters. On the other hand, the new platforms definitively break down borders, thus permitting the expansion of the television industry of some countries (above all the United States) to traditionally closed markets such as China and the Arab countries, in addition to the Eastern European countries that had already been conquered following the fall of the Soviet bloc.

The first two arguments in favour of the regulation of broadcasting media have long been outdated and particular debate surrounds the role of PSB in a society that now possesses a range of alternative media (Tracey 1998).

Two (Historical) Legal Models of Regulation

The varying intensity of state regulation of broadcasting has led to the formation of two models, that of the United States and that of Europe, seen in the literature as being in opposition. Both models are influenced by their differing legal traditions and two different conceptions of public management.

The former expresses the values of liberalism and reflects the US capitalist economic policy, where television was born and developed in a private form, while the latter reflects the history of the European nation-states and the political and economic environment that emerged after the Second World War when public intervention in culture prevailed over freedom of enterprise.

The European public service model has been defined in contradistinction to the market-oriented American model by six features pinpointed by Blumler: ethic of comprehensiveness; generalized mandates; diversity, pluralism and range; cultural vocation; non-commercialism and place in politics (Blumler 1992, pp. 7–21).

These two models no longer exist in their pure form and it is now senseless to study the contrasts between them. However, I will provide a brief description for a comparative historical overview.

Except for rare cases of "State TV," broadcasting systems are mixed, with a predominance of either the public or private sector depending on the legal and cultural traditions of the country.

The relationship between freedom of expression and the structure of the media in the past was fairly linear (public monopoly regimes in Europe and the organization in large networks in the USA). The fall of public monopolies and the emergence—albeit residually—of public TV in the United States as well as in other countries that implemented the US model, have impacted on the characterization of the two historical models.

The few attempts to classify the structural organization of broadcasting enterprises have failed to withstand the test of time. These studies were based on parameters that are no longer relevant, such as the forms of state, especially the contrast between states with a socialist ideology and liberal-democratic states (Terrou and Solal 1951; Debbasch 1995). These Authors proposed subdivisions based on the legal nature of the enterprises (strongly linked to each country's administrative and private law).

An early study looked at both the organization—the *statut de l'entreprise* (code of the enterprise)—and the products of the enterprises, i.e. the output, the boundaries, the criminal implications of information (*statut de la publication* or publication code), which remained generally unchanged for some time and concerned all media. With the arrival of radio and television, however, it became necessary to establish rules relating to the organization that would affect the code of the enterprise (Terrou and Solal 1951, pp. 55–58). Based on the interpretation of constitutional principles, the inquiry proposed a distinction between the (few) systems not based on the subordination of information to political authorities (e.g. Spain, on the basis of the *Fuero*, the law of 17 July 1945; the USSR and its satellite countries) and the (many) systems in which information was subordinated to the political authorities. This premise then gave rise to classification anchored in the code of the enterprise, understood as "the concept of the role of the information and in the formation of any opinion regarding that concept."

The rigid division of broadcasting systems between state monopolies and others not subject to monopoly appeared rather inadequate even when it was proposed. In fact, some scholars observed that there is no great difference between regimes in which the state has a monopoly, but does not directly manage the broadcasting system, and regimes in which the state grants radio and television services to the market but requires that all broadcasters be subject to state authorization.[4]

[4] This was the proposed classification: (1) systems involving a plurality of public and private enterprises (USA, Latin America and Australia); (2) monopolistic or single type systems (the largest group in 1951), further subdivided into 2.1. Enterprises taking the form of commercial companies (Italy, Luxembourg, Finland); 2.2. Enterprises in the form of a

A few decades later, other scholars continued to emphasize the connection between the structural organization and the output, suggesting that the organization is both a reflection of, and the means to achieve: (a) monopoly regimes[5] and (b) pluralistic regimes[6] (Debbasch 1995). Debbasch distinguished between different levels of monopoly, from one in which the state totally controls programmes and broadcasters, to one in which the managing bodies enjoy a certain autonomy. This approach made it possible to identify a broad range of organizational solutions that set the level of connection (or more precisely, of dependence) between the broadcasting body and the state. Even in pluralistic regimes, such pluralism was implemented at different levels: "A l'intérieur de chacune de ces deux catégories, différents degrés de monopole et de pluralisme apparaissent" (Debbasch 1995, p. 11).

Over time, the form of state has proved to be an inadequate indicator of organizational models. Furthermore, even the contraposition between monopolistic and pluralistic regimes has crumbled as the market has

public establishment or office (Germany, Belgium, Romania, Poland); 2.3. Enterprises in the form of a special public service (France, Denmark, Egypt); 2.4. Enterprises in the form of an ordinary public service (Turkey); 2.5. Public enterprises constituted under a single system or placed under a common directorship (Yugoslavia, India); a third case overlapped these two groups; and (3) systems that separated the technical and programme services, granted to one or more companies (Switzerland, Sweden, the Netherlands, Hungary, Bulgaria).

[5] Divided as follows: (1) monopoly conferred on organisms subject to the government such as the "Marxist systems," in which the principle of the "leading role of the communist party" prevented the real autonomy of the broadcasting organizations which were used for propaganda purposes (China, Eastern Europe, former USSR and other countries, until in July 1990, President Mikhail Gorbachev suppressed the control of the CPSU on broadcasting by decree, turning it over to the Government of the Union and then to the Republics; Central and Eastern European countries and Third world countries which, according to the author, were young states in which broadcasting "apparaît comme un excellent moyen d'implantation de l'autorité gouvernementale; elle constitue souvent le seul véhicule culturel utilisable" (p. 22); (2) monopoly exercised by public or semi-public bodies (Italy, Switzerland, The Netherlands, Nordic countries, Ireland, Spain, Portugal, Greece); and (3) monopoly conferred on private companies (Luxembourg and Sweden).

[6] The pluralistic regimes recognize "la nécessité d'une concurrence dans le domaine de la radiodiffusion pour que les libertés d'opinion e d'information soient respectées. Ce pluralisme peut être cependant plus ou moins complet"; on this basis, the group is divided into the following categories: (1) total pluralism (United States, Australia, Canada and Japan) and (2) limited pluralism (characterized by the competition between a certain number of public bodies, in turn having a pluralism of financial origin—United Kingdom-, Federal, like Germany, and cultural: Belgium).

opened to private companies and the principle of pluralism (internal and external) has affirmed itself to varying degrees among all those operating in radio and television.

The fall of the two historical models led to a crisis in the classification of broadcasting systems. Indeed, no classifications have been proposed for years, and legal studies on the subject limit themselves to analyzing individual European legal systems alongside the United States and the existing weak, and rather insignificant, contraposition between the two models.

Undoubtedly, the analysis of the law concerning the organization of European PSB offers a range of organizational solutions that is so broad as to raise doubts as to the efficacy of the classification itself (Chapter 5). It is one of the greatest problems in comparative analysis, namely "many variables, few cases" (Lijphart 1971). However, the situation is not such as to completely exclude any attempt at classification, especially if we avoid using rigid, monothetic categories that are hence directly opposed but prefer a rather more flexible approach.

The US Model

The US model expresses the values of liberalism and reflects the US capitalist economic policy, where television is born and develops in a private form; its rationale can be found in the First Amendment of the Constitution, the pillar on which the democratic system of the US rests: "the Congress shall make no law […] abridging the freedom of speech or of the press."

There has been heated debate by commentators on the absolute or relative value to be attributed to freedom of expression and, consequently on any constraints that may be applied (including state intervention on the media). As the literature has constantly underlined, there is a fine line between restricting freedom of expression and the need to regulate the broadcasting medium to avoid anarchy, thus questioning whether "the regulation of electronic media [has] occurred at the expense of the traditional values of the First Amendment or whether [it is] the reflection of an effort to adapt these values to a new system of technologies" and especially whether it is even harder to define this line when opinions are broadcast "over the air into millions of homes, rather than shouted at the corner of a street" (Botein 1998, p. 292*ff.*). What is at stake here is the defence of the historic concept of the marketplace of ideas that underpins liberal legal thought, whereby ideas emerge and dominate through competition in an environment that permits the free exchange of thought. This vision is summed up in the metaphor proposed by Judge Holmes in his dissenting judgment in the case of *Abrams v. United States* 250 US 616 (1919) where he famously stated "the best test of truth is the power of the thought to get itself accepted in the competition of the market" (for a summary, see Brennen 1982, p. 209; Blocher 2008, p. 821).

Hence, the regulation of broadcasting clearly contrasts with the principles contained in this constitutional provision, and a complex theoretical construction was required to justify state intervention, entrusted both to the legislator and to the Federal Communications Commission (FCC). This latter is an independent agency of the United States government that has proved to be a real market regulator. A key role was played by the Supreme Court that interpreted the Bill of Rights to extend the First Amendment's guarantees to other media by creating a regulatory model (from *Freedman v. Maryland*, 380 US 51, 57 (1965) onwards). The principal reason put forward by the Supreme Court to justify the constitutional legitimacy of broadcasting regulation (on the assumption that freedom of expression does not imply absence of regulation), is the well-known "spectrum scarcity rationale," affirmed in 1943 in *National Broadcasting Co v. United States* and later reiterated in 1969 in *Red Lion Broadcasting Co v. FCC*, a leading case in this sector (*Red Lion Broadcasting Co v. FCC*, 395, US (1969); of the numerous comments, see Firestein 1969, p. 807; Zack 1970, p. 579).

However, not all the actions of those involved in this sector have been inspired by an attempt to ensure this fine balance between freedom of expression and freedom of enterprise. The words of Mark Fowler, Chairman of the FCC, are significant: "The public's interest, then, defines the public interest." The Supreme Court and the FCC have clashed on several occasions, and some of the most decisive moments in US broadcasting history have been marked by the intervention of both, as occurred in the development of the Fairness Doctrine, which profoundly affected broadcasters' activity (among others, see Simmons 1978).

The commercial television model thus reflects the complexity of US law and absorbs its characterizing features: the form of state (although regulation is generally at a federal level, depending on the broadcasting technique, there can also be intervention at state and local levels) the legal system (common law), the constitutional values that characterizes it (with a system that permits forms of self-regulation such as codes of ethics, or regulation through secondary sources of administrative Authorities independent of political power, such as the FCC).

Over almost a century, the US broadcasting system developed like a large commercial machine designed to comply with market logic, and not as a public service. It has been dominated by the various lobbies of the audiovisual industry which have expanded and now cover all the media.

… And Its Circulation

The spread of the US model, especially in Latin America, has essentially been dictated by economic imposition, although there have been examples of a hybrid circulation determined by "prestige" and "voluntary action" (Graziadei 2006, pp. 456–458). However, it would be mistaken to consider Latin America as a homogeneous area of study with a single model (namely commercial TV). Indeed, such a simplistic view would fail to do justice to the Latin American scenario, in which the cultural factor related to each country's political and social fabric fundamentally impacts on the features of their respective broadcasting systems. In the first studies dedicated to the radio, Latin America was set alongside the United States in the classification that contemplates the cases of the plurality of public and private enterprises (Terrou and Solal 1951, p. 138).

To better understand the instance of systems that do not immediately align with the US model, we should consider the typical elements of this model that we find in the Latin American broadcasting systems. Moreover, we should ascertain whether the circulation of the US model has been uniform, or if each state has partially incorporated this model while adding its own characteristics. Finally, we should ascertain whether there are common (and determining) elements that characterize the Latin American broadcasting systems that may confirm a generalized deviation from the US model.

As regards this last point, there are clearly some recurrent features in the history of many Latin American countries, certain "cryptotypes"[7]

[7] Cryptotypes are implicit models, present in different legal systems, that act in a pervasive way in the determination of legal issues and are transmitted through generations of jurists (Sacco 1992, p. 128).

that have influenced each country's constitutional path and have also affected the development of their broadcasting systems. To cite the most evident and recurrent features, I refer to the power exerted by the military and the rise of authoritarian governments seen in most of these countries, and even on several occasions within the same country.[8] I refer also to the particular system of presidential government, which has affected the relations between politics and television,[9] as well as the economic domination of the United States which has sometimes promoted the two expressions of power mentioned above (through support to the military governments or the pro-American politics of some Presidents).

[8]The *extra ordinem* governments exercised a control of freedom expression both as regards substance (censorship, determination of the contents of broadcasts for propaganda purposes, etc.) and structure (governmental appointment of the top management bodies of the broadcasters). This was the case in Argentina during the dictatorship of General Lanusse, in 1972 with the nationalization of the private radio and television channels and in 1975 with the law on the expropriation of television channels relating to both repeaters and production (Muraro 1987); in Brazil, from the military coup of 1964–1984, in the twenty years in which several military governments succeeded each other, TV was controlled to dominate public opinion (in the first period of the *mariscal* Castelo Branco—1964–1966—the *Empresa Brasileira de Telecomunicações* (Embratel) was set up and the contract with the US Time-Life group was cancelled; in the second period of the *mariscal* Costa and Silva (1966–1968) institutional law n. 5 on the suppression of freedom of expression in the country was approved; for other periods: Capparelli and dos Santos 2002, pp. 77–78).

[9]In Latin America, the relationship between politics and radio–television must be contextualized in a specific authoritarian declination of the form of presidential government implemented without (or with a strong attenuation) of that system of checks and balances affirmed in the USA to compensate for the excessive power (on paper) of the President. The presidential influence has manifested itself in different ways: from the holding of shares in radio and television groups by former Presidents (as for Miguel Alemán in Mexico), to the personal and direct management of agreements with the largest foreign corporations—above all from the USA—for the issuing of licences (as in Chile, before the military coup of 1973, with government decree 7039/1958) this became an actual tool for trading votes (in Brazil, the expression "coronelismo electrónico" is used to describe the relationship of political cronyism between those holding power in the public sphere and the owners of television stations, a particularly significant phenomenon in the period of transition from military regimes to the new democratic phase. What happened in Mexico is a clear example of this particular relationship between politics and TV: the constant union between the *Partido Revolucionario Institucional* (PRI) and the television (fundamentally represented by a private operator: *Televisa*) is summed up in the expression "Televisa fue a los medios electrónico lo que el Partido Revolucionario Institucional (PRI) fue al sistema político mexicano" (Fernández 2002, p. 17).

Despite the presence of these elements, which are common to many Latin American countries and which distance them from the historical, political and cultural environment in which US commercial TV formed, the broadcasting landscape is not homogeneous and witnesses the presence of a number of historical models (i.e. different experiences in the birth of broadcasting systems, rather than exportable prototypes). The genesis of individual broadcasting systems evidences a contrast. On the one hand, we have countries where television was born as public TV or, more precisely, state TV such as Venezuela, Colombia, Argentina and Peru, with Chile as a major example.[10] On the other hand, there are countries such as Brazil, where the birth of television was marked by private initiative and a culture of profit in a sector conceived more as an industry than as a vehicle of education, knowledge and, more generally of broadcasting with a public mission. In the latter case, the commercial TV model dominates and is rooted in the earliest radio broadcasting.

The mosaic of Latin American models thus includes:

a. a model of commercial TV that predominated from the beginning (e.g. Brazil, Mexico and later Venezuela);
b. a mixed model (public and private with some constraints), which now operates alongside a classic expression of commercial TV that has become firmly established only in the last decade (Colombia);
c. an exception to the spread of commercial TV in the Latin American area, represented by Chilean public TV which, if nothing else, frustrates any attempt to place the Latin American systems in a single large class ascribable to the US model.

[10] In Chile, television became established at the end of the 1950s, later than in the other countries on the continent, mainly as public TV of the universities (secular or Catholic) unlike the radio that was born with private companies. In the initial phase, private TV played a marginal role in the broadcasting system and the great American giants remained of relative importance thanks to the development of public TV (Fuenzalida 1984). The reasons were economic (there was no tradition of large private national companies in the communications sector); cultural (the public and private university system was very prestigious and "had a well-developed cultural infrastructure [...] such as theatres, symphony orchestras, choirs, dance groups, cinema, bookshops and publishing houses": Fuenzalida 2002, p. 164) and political (on the one hand, university television was considered as a maximum guarantee of political and ideological pluralism; on the other hand, some Presidents were decisive in the policy of excluding private commercial television, that was considered unsuitable for upholding the cultural role that the country required).

The US model has therefore circulated thanks to the formidable vehicle of economic development rather than to any inherent prestige; the big Networks worked their way into the local market thanks to agreements with (often small) national broadcasters. On the organizational side too, the juxtaposition of the Latin American television companies to the US Networks appears forced.

Therefore, when studying the Latin American television systems, it is important to highlight the cultural elements and political factors that typify each state, and which have contributed to characterize the individual experiences. In this (cultural) area, certain cryptotypes emerge that determine: the pre-eminent use of certain sources (e.g. government decrees, normative acts adopted in emergency situations by authoritarian governments or presidential acts in democratic regimes); the limited relevance of regional TV in proportion to the decentralized form of state (more precisely, federal) in many states; and the regulation of public TV, where this exists, that is subject to interference from the political class (especially the President).

In fact, political influence and varying levels and forms of governmental control over the broadcasting media were most frequently exercised by the countries' Presidents, even when the regime was not authoritarian.

The form of patronage, typical of these legal systems, has little in common with the American commercial television environment. It is, however, true that in the history of US broadcasting, there have been times when the FCC (but not the government!) was accused of cronyism in the issuing of licences granted with non-transparent criteria that did not pursue the public interest or follow market logic.

Such a logic of exchange seems closer to that witnessed in the European model prevalent in the Mediterranean area than the US liberal model. The development of Latin American Countries has not given rise to the same cultural environment that led to the implementation of freedom of speech being entrusted to the market in the USA, to avoid state control/interference.

On the other hand, this area does not have the same shared legal and cultural tradition surrounding public service that exists in the European Countries. The Latin American Countries are clearly lacking as regards the structural and organizational development of a public service, though it may sometimes be present regarding content and mission, especially in the cases of Chile and Colombia. Furthermore, most political attention has been directed towards private television. In the few cases in which the state has invested in public TV, politics has also exercised a certain influence, as was the case in Colombia.

The Birth of the European Model: The BBC

In contrast to the United States, the model that emerged in Europe was influenced by the history of the Nation-states and the political and economic context resulting in the aftermath of the Second World War.

A series of common interests and values that extended beyond a simple refusal of a commercial TV model, meant that states differed for many aspects, yet shared the idea of public service and the common mission with which it should be entrusted.

The shared idea was that of the public broadcasting service as a "normative, as well as a descriptive, concept," whose characteristics have been effectively summarized by the scholarship in six key points: "1. general geographical availability; 2. concern for national identity and culture; 3. independence from both the state and commercial interests; 4. impartiality of programmes; 5. range and variety of programmes; and 6. substantial financing by a general charge on users" (Barendt 1995, p. 52).

The formation of this *idem sentire* derives from the circulation of a cultural model that was born with the BBC in Britain and developed on three pillars that were defined from the outset by its first Director General, Sir John Reith: information, entertainment and education. "To have exploited so great a scientific invention for the purpose and pursuit of 'entertainment' alone would have been a prostitution of its powers and an insult to the character and intelligence of the people," commented Reith in his book Broadcast over Britain (Reith 1924, p. 17).

The target contemplated by Reith was the people (not the advertising market), the mission went beyond mere entertainment and, consequently, the organizational structure was influenced by the weight of this mandate. The choice of removing the broadcasting system from the play of the free market to entrust it to the hands of the public was taken up in the recommendations of the early Inquiry Committees, and later enshrined in the legislative texts (Hibberd 2005), but see also, at least, the work of the British historian Briggs (1961), Burns (1977), and Coase (1950).

From the founding of the BBC, the Inquiry Committees clearly outlined the public broadcaster's profile, by rejecting the US model: The Crawford Committee judged any solution based on a total and uncontrolled freedom of broadcasting and reception to be unsuitable for Britain and preferred a public body as, the Committee believed, any company or organization established for profit would be inadequate (Crawford Committee, *Report of the Broadcasting Committee*, presented to Parliament on 2 March 1926).

As regards the organizational form, these values translated into the following axiom: independence of the broadcasting corporation from the State (public but not state TV!) and the market.

In legal terms, this was reflected in some requirements related to:

- sources. The broadcasting sector is regulated by the laws of the Westminster Parliament on communications, but a Royal Charter was chosen for the BBC that was formally approved by the Monarch on the basis of the royal prerogative (a residual power that still belongs to the Crown and is thus actually exercised by the government). The Royal Charter defines the objectives of the BBC, establishes the responsibilities of the corporation and its bodies and envisages a licence fee as the source of funding. It is accompanied by an Agreement (a contract between the BBC and the government), which defines public service obligations. The first Royal Charter dates back to 1927 and the last one was issued in 2017;
- the nature of the corporation (see the Sykes and Crawford Inquiry Committees);
- the internal bodies (the Board of Governors and the Director General, which lasted for more than 80 years; the Trust (Royal Charter 2007) and a new Board (Royal Charter 2017);
- the method of funding (through a licence fee, with no advertising);
- the imposition of a series of obligations on private television operators falling within the concept of public service, albeit with some differences with respect to the BBC. The history of British broadcasting is marked also by an early opening to the market that was strongly opposed by those who had established the public service.[11] The 1954 Television Act created the first commercial Network: Independent Television (ITV), later known as Channel 3, as well as the Independent Television Authority (ITA), the first regulatory body for commercial television.[12]

[11] John Reith, in his address to the House of Lords on 22 May 1952, compared the introduction of commercial broadcasting to smallpox, the bubonic plague and the Black Death (Briggs 1961, p. 397*ff.*). The fierce opposition to the introduction of commercial TV was driven by the fear of diminishing the high level of quality ensured until then in the BBC broadcasts (see Craufurd Smith 1997, p. 38 and the bibliography to that effect mentioned therein).

[12] This is a Network of local broadcasters (a sort of confederation of television companies committed to countering the excessive attention that the BBC devoted to the London area), financed exclusively through the sale of advertising space. It is required to guarantee

The "comfortable duopoly" lasted until the approval of the Broadcasting Act of 1980, which established Channel 4, a nonprofit public corporation financed with commercial resources, whose mandate focused predominantly on programmes for minorities created through contracts with independent producers.[13]

Subsequently, the public service broadcasters were expanded with the addition of Channel 5 (later Five), formed by a consortium of British publishers and granted the fifth television licence in 1995 with a rather limited mandate, given the exquisitely commercial nature of the programming.

Until the Broadcasting Act of 1990, the distinction between public TV and private TV in the UK was based purely on economic criteria (financing with or without advertising), with all Commercial Public Service Broadcasting being subject to public service constraints, similar to those that Reith had created for the BBC. The 1990 law, which favoured a certain liberalization of the sector, increased the gap between the two types of television. The spread of cable and satellite TV then led to a broadening of the television offer and the emergence of broadcasters that were not subject to public service obligations, but still required to comply with certain standards established by the codes of conduct (based on respect for values including good taste, a sense of decency, impartiality and truthfulness of information).[14]

The unusual legal situation in which the BBC operates can only be understood within the context of the British system, where there is a tradition of constitutional debate (and consensus) on the objectives of public TV and its relationship with the state and the public (Chapter 6).

diversified programming that includes a national information service and local programming. ITV began broadcasting on 22 September 1955 in the London area, and after four years the service covered the whole territory of the British Isles.

[13]Confirmed by the 2003 Communications Act: in addition to the generic obligations related to high-quality programmes, Channel 4 is required to demonstrate "innovation, experiment and creativity" in the form and content of programmes, as well as to exhibit 'a distinctive character, and to provide educational programming': see S. 265(3).

[14]The 2003 Communications Act provides, in fact, a "layered" regulation of the broadcasters' mandate: the first concerns the aforementioned standards, applicable to all radio and television broadcasters; the second includes obligations that burden all the broadcasters belonging to the PSB in a quantitatively different proportion (quotas for independent programming, for educational programmes, etc.); the third refers to qualitative obligations (in general, to provide high-quality programming and diversity of content).

Over the years, the BBC has been able to create a tradition of PSB, in compliance with obligations coming not from the legislator, but debated and agreed at every renewal of the Royal Charter (an occasion that always involves a profound reflection on the organization of the entire national broadcasting system). The text submitted to the Queen and the Parliament is inspired by the work of the Committees appointed by the Minister. Even though the Committee members are chosen by the government, each of the Committees formed since 1923 has tackled the key themes of the broadcasting system with independence, advancing highly innovative proposals. Some, but not all, of the various Committees' proposals have been included in the final charter, confirming their impartiality. For example, the final report of the Peacock Commission, appointed in 1986, during the Thatcher era, opted against privatization and the use of advertising in contrast to the wishes of the government of the time.

Even when faced with the challenges of technological development, the BBC has not abdicated its mission but has responded by modernizing. In the 2007 Charter, six goals were incorporated to strengthen the mission of the public broadcaster. Furthermore, a public test value was envisaged for the new services and significant changes were introduced for those already operational (with an expansion of the offer of both programmes and thematic channels). The author of the digital strategy that led the BBC to modernize and remain competitive was the then Director General John Birt (now Lord Birt), who was responsible for the first six channels broadcast by a single digital terrestrial multiplex.[15] The BBC is well known as a public broadcaster, but it can also be considered as a provider of public service interactivity (PSI) (Bracken and Balfour 2002, p. 99*ff.*).

… And Its Circulation Outside Europe

The British experience has contributed to the emergence of a model that has spread throughout Europe, often thanks to judgments passed down through the Constitutional Courts (see Chapter 4). In addition, it has sometimes spread beyond the borders of Europe, influencing some Western-style democracies that are too often hastily categorized as belonging to a commercial TV model along the lines of that of the

[15] To BBC1 and BBC2, the channels of general interest, were added BBC Choice—for a younger audience with a time slot for children called CBBC—; BBC News 24; BBC Parliament and BBCi, an interactive teletext service.

United States (see the classifications of the French study mentioned above). While this may be correct when explaining the genesis of these broadcasting systems and the economic and cultural influences exerted by the US model on those broadcasting markets, the principles and values that still hold for the European model are present in those countries where PSB contributes to fulfilling important state purposes (promotion of ethnic minorities, protection of bilingualism, etc.).

In Canada, for example, the broadcasting system is mixed and is affected by both cultural models; the British model was the inspiration for the public body of the Canadian Broadcasting Corporation (CBC), created in 1936 as a national radio service in response to the invasion of the Canadian airwaves by the emerging US networks. The linguistic factor fundamentally affects the organization of the public service. In fact, CBC is divided into two main networks: CBC Television in English and Télévision de Radio-Canada in French. Both networks are charged with producing programmes that must be "principally and distinctly Canadian," ensuring "equivalent quality" in the two languages and that (despite the unusual nature of this federal state), must "contribute to spreading awareness and national identity." Public broadcasting is exclusively of federal jurisdiction, the Canadian Provinces have their own broadcasters and operate through a grant from the Federal Government. It is noteworthy that each must have an "educational channel" (for further information on the legislation: Grant and Buchanan 2016).

Frequently, the focus on PSB is the legacy of British culture on former colonies, as in Australia, where the BBC model has deeply affected the public network both as regards the mission (structured to favour minorities) and the organizational–structural aspect (a good starting point is Armstrong 1982). Commercial TV is still predominant and, in part, identifies the Australian experience, but the public service needs are fulfilled by two different categories of broadcasters in line with the original classification of the Broadcasting Services Act 1992. The first is the "community broadcasting," originally labelled as "public broadcasting" which was started in the 1970s to meet the needs of local communities or specific sectors within these and providing a service that was much more similar to US public broadcasting (it represents the interests of particular categories of society, is financed by contributions from the civil society itself and does not transmit commercial advertising). The second, called the national broadcasting service, is entrusted to two separate entities: the Australian Broadcasting Corporation (ABC), created in

1928 as a network of pre-existing private radio stations, and the Special Broadcasting Service Corporation (SBC), established in 1975 specifically to provide multilingual and multicultural radio and television services. Both have legal status as public corporations and are exempt from licencing by the Australian Broadcasting Authority (ABA). Only the parts of the Broadcasting Services Act expressly specified apply to these two corporations, because the reference source is a Charter adopted by the Federal Parliament, within the framework of a specific legislation for the individual broadcasters. For years the structural organization of these two Australian public broadcasters reflected that of the BBC's Board of Governors (with a Board of Directors made up of a Managing Director and a variable number (4–8) of non-executive Directors who may serve for no more than two consecutive five-year periods and are appointed by the Governor-General on the basis of experience gained also in the multicultural sector). Scholars have noted that the organization and the source chosen for regulating these corporations (a Charter) share the same characteristic of independence that underlies the BBC (Hitchens 2006, especially Ch. 3, p. 63*ff*).

The public service imprint of the European model can also be recognized when it is not the companies themselves that are supported but the output, as in New Zealand. In this case, the state intervenes to offset market failure in order to cover areas that would not be reached by private enterprise. Due to the high costs of covering the entire territory caused by the country's orographic features, commercial stations have contributed to the functioning of the public broadcaster since the 1930s by devolving part of their commercial revenues. Moreover, such means were necessary as the low population meant that the licence fee was inadequate to meet the costs (Burrows and Cheer 2005; Cocker 1994). The New Zealand Broadcasting Corporation—inspired by the BBC—broadcasted from the late 1960s to 1989, when the conservative government of the National Party transformed it into a private company with no public service obligations on the market like any other Commercial TV. The only public broadcasting constraint was covered by the independent Broadcasting Commission (better known as New Zealand On Air), set up with the Broadcasting Act of 1989. New Zealand On Air manages the funding granted to TVNZ for the production of cultural and local programmes for the country's public. In 1999, given the inability of TVNZ to respond to the needs of minorities and supply adequate output, the Telecommunications Minister Marian Hobbs of the governing Labour Party, initiated the process of reintroducing PSB (Lealand 2008, p. 149*ff*). In September 2000, a draft statute was published reflecting the interests of the Maori, minors and other groups and in 2003 the final version was approved. This document was strongly inspired by the BBC and resembled the founding acts of Australian and Canadian PSB, with a particular focus on the minorities. This unusual return to public service marks the New Zealand case as an interesting alternative experience of support for PSB.

The European model and, especially that of the BBC, has also influenced Countries with different traditions, such as Japan. The Japanese public broadcaster, Nippon HĐsĐ KyĐkai (NHK) has grown into possibly the world's best-funded public service broadcasting organization thanks to the payment by users of a licence fee and is also a major pioneer of digital TV. Moreover, despite an eclectic mix of obligations, it is one of the leading interpreters of the public service mission and programming decisions have been in line with the demands of the audience while maintaining strong traditional PSB values (Priebs 2002, p. 121).

The Evolution of PSB: From Monopoly to PSB 2.0

It is useful to trace the history of the European model of PSB as it developed through a series of phases to better understand the evolution in the relationship between PSB and politics.

As Donders states (Donders 2012, p. 9), some scholars make a distinction between two phases: the period before and after liberalization (e.g. Levy 1999; Michalis 2007); others make a distinction between three phases: the monopoly, liberalization and digital age (e.g. Collins et al. 2001; Leurdijk 2007).

If we emphasize the legislative and jurisprudential interventions that have characterized the development of state public broadcasters, we note that the "liberalization" phase was preceded by a separate period, that of the "modernization" of the radio and television sector, which preceded the actual fall of the monopolies.

- In the first historical phase, the intervention of the state took the form of direct management of broadcasting activity through the monopoly (*de iure* and de facto), due to the technical, economic, cultural and political topics discussed earlier. In this phase, the presence (and influence) of political power (or more correctly, of the government) in the organization and activity of the managing body meant, among other things, the appointment of managing bodies and control on programming. In the Western European democracies, broadcasting was organized as a service that could be used to spread and guarantee the pluralism of political opinions. On the other hand, in the Eastern European Countries, and in Spain and Portugal, up to the mid-1970s, the monopoly facilitated propaganda and information control. The only exception in Europe was Luxembourg that did not establish public broadcasting, but a private broadcasting enterprise that was, in fact, a private monopoly until 1991.

- The second phase of liberalization was preceded by a period of "modernization" of the broadcasting sector (1960s–1970s). The new relationship between the state and citizens led to a review of the institutions that were charged with important tasks such as communication and information. Although the new Constitutions did not contain a direct reference to television, they contained a series of principles that inevitably impacted on broadcasting activities (pluralism of information, protection of minorities, etc.). The monopoly, as conceived and organized up to that moment (with a strong dependence on government power), was no longer suitable to pursue the public interest expressed in the new Constitutions. However, it remained a tool for the spread of the socialist ideology in the countries of Eastern Europe. The European legislators tried to combine the constitutional guarantees on freedom of expression with state intervention through a reconfiguration of their public broadcasters. To this end, the state presence (person and apparatus) was "redesigned" to encompass civil society (the Netherlands) and regional autonomy (Germany and Belgium). Furthermore, the role of the government was reduced in favour of Parliament that was considered the most suitable constitutional body to exercise control over PSB. From then onwards, the nature of PSB was Janus-faced as, on the one hand, it was tasked with guaranteeing freedom of expression on the other hand, it required a series of guarantees to defend itself against the interference of its owner, i.e. the state.

The phase of liberalization swept through the Western European broadcasting systems with a domino effect, leading to the revival of market-led policies at the expense of interventionist government policies (Dyson and Humphreys 1988, p. 92*ff.*).

However, during the transition, the process of abandonment of the monopolies differed in the different European countries. In some cases, the intervention of the Constitutional Courts was fundamental and substituted the role of the legislator (Italy); in other cases, such intervention steered a legislator whose response could be long in coming (Spain). By contrast, the transition to a mixed system often took place promptly by legislative means (France and the UK). Sometimes the fall of the monopolies was triggered by foreign broadcasters who were pushing to enter the national market rather than by internal market pressures (Scandinavian countries).

Several private radio and television broadcasters, often owned by powerful groups with commercial interests in several countries and in different sectors of communication, appeared alongside the public broadcasters.[16]

The new opportunities for private enterprise had significant repercussions on public broadcasters, both at a cultural and legal level. It was necessary to update the law to regulate new aspects such as broadcaster licencing, service obligations as well as the establishment of independent administrative authorities for regulation and supervision in the broadcasting and/or telecommunications sector and so forth.

- In the phase known as the digital age, that saw a shift to Public Service Media (PSM), even those who supported the preservation of PSB agreed on the need to redefine its characteristics in order to conserve the historical heritage of knowledge acquired by PSB in the communication sector (Barnett 2007; Jakubowicz 2007). "Public service broadcasting institutions might be struggling in the face of fierce competition, deregulation, audience fragmentation and technological transformation, but in most European countries they are still regarded as integral parts of their respective countries' cultural and democratic welfare [...]. In Europe, the flame of PSB still burns relatively brightly where in many other countries it barely flickers" (Barnett 2007, p. 89).

[16]For a snapshot of enterprises currently operating in the television market directly or through shareholdings in larger groups: *Yearbook. Film, television and video in Europe*, published by the European Audiovisual Observatory of the Council of Europe, latest version (as well as the *Mavise* Database that can be accessed on http://mavise.obs.coe.int/).

Nowadays, communication policy is enacted within a multilateral system of governance; numerous binding and non-binding international bodies still affirm the need for a free and plural media and have cited PSB as a way to achieve this (e.g. the importance of cultural diversity is carried on by UNESCO through the policy of diversity of the media of the states).[17]

There are many reasons to rethink PSB and turn it into PSM or preferably perhaps to set PSB at the core of PSM (Donders 2012, p. 43). Several times, European institutions have reaffirmed the relevance of PSB in the new digital era and the importance for PSB to develop online media service. They support the expansion of PSB into the online world "within the constraints of the regulatory framework developed by European Commission decisions on state Aid and by the Court of Justice of the European Union" (Brevini 2013, p. 18). The development of PSB online has encouraged scholars to propose a model for PSB 2.0 that "is not limited to a technocratic definition that might relate it just to PSB online services boosted by the participation architecture of Web 2.0," but "is constructed as a policy arrangement based on a set of normative values that derive from a revised definition of PSB that can extend to the online world" (Brevini 2013, p. 18). The new scenario offered by digital technology and the Web, therefore, requires new arguments and new criteria for regulation of PSB according to the whole spectrum of public life (Scannell 1989).

In Europe, two apparently conflicting trends in regulation coexist.

At the external, supranational level, the Council of Europe and European Commission, though using different tools and with different purposes, both tend to reinforce the importance of PSB and urge the states to adopt regulations that are as homogeneous as possible and comply with the principles of pluralism and media independence (Donders and Pauwels 2008) (see Chapter 3).

[17]UNESCO Convention on the Protection and the Promotion of the Diversity of Cultural Expressions of 2007 that allows states to adopt measures aimed not only at protecting and promoting the diversity of cultural expressions "within its territory (Art. 6.1)", "but specifically at enhancing the diversity of the media including through public service broadcasting" (Art. 6.2.h).

At a national level, many states have initiated a debate on the role of PSB, on the way it might be financed and, more generally, on the governance of public broadcasters. The tendency has been, however, to undertake slight reform that influences the internal organization rather than the entire sector (see Chapter 6). Few countries stand out for implementing and investing in online PSB (the exception being the UK).

As regards the mission and remits, a prototype of PSB that complies with these principles has now risen like a phoenix from the cultural model of the BBC, "sifted" from the ashes by the supranational organizations and based on a series of pan-European standards welcomed by national legislatures (Pavani 2016, p. 29). While the future of technological development and the new scenario of online PSB remains uncertain, the importance of the BBC online framework is unquestionable. This has led commentators to wonder whether a new model of online PSB will be more affected by the European influence or BBC policy transfer (Chapter 3).

Several (Heuristic) Cultural Models

Having described the two (historical), legal models of regulation, based on the predominantly legal parameters, I wish to discuss some (heuristic) cultural models, created by scholars of other social sciences.

Such models can be useful when carrying out a legal analysis of the organization of PSB, for sorting the data collected according to criteria that measure the relationship between the political system and the media system and, specifically, between the political system and PSB. This is particularly useful in the study of the organization and governance of PSB.

As in the legal field, most of the literature on the media "is highly ethnocentric, in the sense that it refers only to the experience of a single country, yet is written in general terms, as though the model that prevailed in that country were universal" (Hallin and Mancini 2004, p. 2).

However, there is a continuing current of comparative scholarship dating back to the 1950s with studies on the press (Siebert et al. 1956) that decades later crops up in research into broadcasting, and investigates the relationship between media and politics and how the two influence each other, as well as why media vary profoundly between one country and another.

One study, in particular, proposed three models of media systems: the North Atlantic or Liberal Model; the North-Central European or Democratic Corporatist Model; the Mediterranean or Polarized Pluralist Model (Hallin and Mancini 2004); this investigation inspired further analyses of broadcasting systems (e.g. Terzis 2007).[18]

The comparative approach of these studies "makes the invisible visible" and emphasizes certain aspects of the communication systems that "may be taken for granted, and [are] difficult to detect when the focus is only on the case of a single nation" (Blumler and Gurevitch 1995, p. 76).

The models were created by taking into account four macro-criteria: the development of the media market, with particular attention to press circulation; the so-called "Political parallelism," referring to the relationship between the media and political parties, or more generally, "the way and the level at which the communication system reflects the main existing political divisions in society"; the development of professional journalism and the degree and nature of state intervention in the media system.

Their models are intended as empirical, not normative models: scholars are not interested "in measuring media systems against a normative ideal, but in analysing their historical development as institutions within particular social settings" (Hallin and Mancini 2004, p. 14).

The liberal model that prevails in the UK, Ireland and North America is characterized by the predominance of commercial media and by the habit of always reasoning in terms of "Anglo-American journalism." However, this model shows a strong dissociation between radio and television (public, par excellence, in the UKand Ireland and commercial in the United States) and other media.

The democratic corporatist model has become established in continental Europe and is characterized by a strong cohesion between the media and social groups (trade unions, religious organizations, cultural and political movements). In these countries, television is a particularly important example of the logic of the social state applied to the media.

The Mediterranean model encompasses countries such as Italy, Spain, Greece and Portugal as well as France, although the latter is often treated as a marginal case compared to other countries. It is

[18] This study divides the Countries by areas according to the classification of Hallin and Mancini, to which it adds the countries of Eastern Europe (The Eastern European/Post-communist Media Model Countries, p. 303*ff.*).

characterized by a strong link between media and politics; a low circulation of newspapers and an elite press; a high level of political parallelism, especially in the television sector; strong state intervention that manifests itself in various ways (economic subsidies to the press in Italy and France, strong deregulation, preventive controls on some media).

The study shows that the influences of a country's political system and political history on media development are particularly noticeable in countries belonging to the Mediterranean model, in which "the mass media [...] were intimately involved in the political conflicts that mark the history of this region, and there is a strong tradition of regarding them as a means of ideological expression and political mobilization."

These countries are characterized by a high level of political parallelism, as demonstrated by a study in which this criterion is applied to PSB. As noted, "the extent of politicisation of the public-service broadcasters varied very considerably. Different political systems presented varying opportunities for it to occur and encouraged different manifestations of it" (Humphreys 1996, pp. 145–146). Depending on the strength of the link between PSB and the state, this study identifies four models of public broadcasters: governmental, professional, parliamentary and corporatist. The construction of these models is based on a partly diachronic analysis of certain paradigmatic countries, although no actual comparative or transversal study is attempted. However, the elements characterizing the models are useful for understanding some of the dynamics related to the governance of PSB.

The governmental model unites various state experiences in the early phase of the development of public monopoly; France is emblematic of this model, where broadcasters operate within a centralized, statist and majoritarian polity. The experiences of Portugal, Spain and Greece also fall within this model.

The professional model is symbolized by the BBC and has spread to countries influenced by the British experience, such as Canada and Ireland, but also to the Scandinavian countries.

The parliamentary model is characterized by a control over PSB split between the political parties. Italy is the prime example, along with other countries of Mediterranean Europe that share a culture of clientelism (Humphreys 1996, p. 157).

The civic or corporatist model is based on a consensual system combining politicization with political pluralism: in Germany and Austria, there existed a tradition of inter-party cooperation, while the model of the Netherlands is based on the pillars.

Hallin and Mancini then combine the four models developed by Humphreys with a further classification of broadcasting systems based on the political influence proposed by Kelly: politics-over-broadcasting systems; formally autonomous systems and politics-in-broadcasting systems (Kelly 1983, pp. 65–82). The professional model should be a formally autonomous system; the governmental model should be a politics-over-broadcasting system; the parliamentary and the civic models should be a politics-in-the-broadcasting system. For the purposes of the analysis of the link between PSB and the political system, the authors stress that "the professional, parliamentary, and civic/corporatist models are all, in some sense, solutions to the problem of how to keep public broadcasting, or a regulatory authority, from falling under the control of the most powerful political force and failing to serve a politically diverse society."

Conclusion

From the outset, the (few) attempts to classify the structure and organization of broadcasting systems showed limitations. The rigid taxonomy based on the legal nature of the broadcaster—and on the form of state as a meta-parameter—immediately appeared inadequate. The comparative analysis of circulation of these two models confirms the weakness of this approach. In fact, many of the countries frequently ascribed to a model based on the prestige or economic imposition of the dominant country, in fact, present elements that are relevant to the alternative model. This was clearly evidenced in this Chapter through the discussion on the Latin-American experiences and comparison with the US model.

As noted, the cultural element of public TV (though not state TV) of the European Model circulated beyond the borders of Europe to some Western-style democracies that are frequently and hastily categorized as belonging to a commercial TV model along the lines of the US model. The model of Public Service Broadcasting that has emerged and spread in Europe itself has been considerably influenced by the British experience, often thanks to judgments passed down through the Constitutional Courts. These principles still influence the evolution of PSB in the digital age and the importance of the BBC online framework is unquestionable. Many commentators now wonder whether a new model of online PSB will be affected more by the European influence or by BBC policy transfer.

The reference to some (heuristic) cultural models, created by scholars of other social sciences, can help to measure the relationship between the political system and the media system and, specifically, between the political system and PSB (see Chapters 6 and 7).

References

Armstrong, M. (1982). *Broadcasting law and policy in Australia*. Sydney: Butterworths.

Baggaley, J. P., & Duck, S.W. (1977). *Dynamics of television*. Lexington: Lexington Books.

Barendt, E. (1995). *Broadcasting law: A comparative study*. Oxford: Oxford University Press.

Barendt, E., & Hitchens, L. (2000). *Media law, cases and materials*. Harlow: Longman.

Barnett, S. (2007). Can the public service broadcaster survive? Renewal and compromise in the new BBC Charter. In G. Ferrel Lowe & J. Bardoel (Eds.), *From public service broadcasting to public service media*. Gothenburg: Nordicom.

Bollinger, L. C. (1976). Freedom of the press and public access: Toward a theory of partial regulation. *Michigan Law Review, 75*(1), 1–42.

Blocher, J. (2008). Institutions in the marketplace of ideas. *Duke Law Journal, 57*, 821–889.

Blumler, J. G. (1991). *Broadcasting finance in transition: A comparative handbook*. Oxford: Oxford University Press.

Blumler, J. G. (1992). *Television and the public interest*. London: Sage.

Blumler, J. G., & Gurevitch, M. (1995). *The crisis of public communication*. London: Routledge.

Botein, M. (1998). *Regulation of the electronic mass media: Law and policy for radio, television, cable and the new video technologies* (3rd ed.). Saint Paul: West Group Publishing.

Bracken, M., & Balfour, A. (2002). Public service interactivity and the BBC. In J. Cowling & D. Tambini (Eds.), *From public service broadcasting to public service communications*. London: Institute for Public Policy Research.

Brennen, D. L. (1982). A marketplace of ideas approach to broadcast regulation. *Texas Law Review, 60*, 207–257.

Brevini, B. (2013). *Public service broadcasting online: A comparative European policy study of PSB 2.0*. London: Palgrave Macmillan.

Briggs, A. (1961). *The history of broadcasting in the United Kingdom, Volume one: The birth of broadcasting*. Oxford: Oxford University Press.

Burns, T. (1977). *The BBC: Public institution and private world*. London: Macmillan.

Burrows, J., & Cheer, U. (2005). *Media law in New Zealand*. South Melbourne: Oxford University Press.
Capparelli, S., & dos Santos, S. (2002). La televisión en Brasil. In G. Orozco (Ed.), *Historias de la televisión en América Latina*. Barcelona: Gedisa.
Coase, R. H. (1950). *British broadcasting: A study in monopoly*. New York: Routledge.
Cocker, A. (1994). Broadcasting myths and political realities: New Zealand's experience in comparative perspective. *Political Science, 46*(2), 234–254.
Collins, R., Finn, A., McFayden, S., & Hoskin, C. (2001). Public service broadcasting beyond 2000: Is there a future for public service broadcasting? *Canadian Journal of Communication, 26*(1), 3–15.
Craufurd Smith, R. (1997). *Broadcasting law and fundamental rights*. Oxford: Oxford University Press.
Debbasch, C. (1995). *Droit de l'audiovisuel*. Paris: Dalloz.
Dyson, K., & Humphreys, P. (1988). Regulatory change in Western Europe: From national cultural regulation to international economic statecraft. In K. Dyson & P. Humphreys (Eds.), *Broadcasting and new media policies in Western Europe*. London: Routledge.
Donders, K. (2012). *Public service media and policy in Europe*. New York: Palgrave Macmillan.
Donders, K., & Pauwels, C. (2008). Does EU policy challenge the digital future of public service broadcasting? An analysis of the Commission's state aid approach to digitization and the public service remit of public broadcasting organizations. *Convergence: The International Journal of Research into New Media Technologies, 14*(3), 295–311.
Fernández, F. (2002). *La responsabilidad de los medios de comunicación*. México: Paidós.
Firestein, L. C. (1969). Red Lion and the fairness doctrine: Regulation of broadcasting in the public interest. *11 Arizona Law Review*, 807–820.
Fuenzalida, V. (1984). *Estudios sobre la Televisión Chilena*. Santiago: CPU.
Fuenzalida, V. (2002). La Televisión en Chile. In G. Orozco (Coord.), *Historias de la televisión en América Latina*. Barcelona: Gedisa.
Garnham, N. (1990). *Capitalism and communication: Global culture and the economics of information*. London: Sage.
Gibbons, T. (1998). *Regulating the media*. London: Sweet & Maxwell.
Goldberg, D., Prosser, T., & Verhulst, S. (1998). *Regulating the changing media: A comparative study*. Oxford: Clarendon Press.
Goldberg, D., Sutter, G., & Walden, I. (Eds.). (2009). *Media law and practice*. Oxford: Oxford University Press.
Grant, P. S., & Buchanan, G. (2016). *Canadian broadcasting regulatory handbook* (13th ed.). Toronto: McCarthy Tétrault.

Graziadei, M. (2006). Comparative law as the study of transplants and receptions. In M. Reimann & M. Zimmermann (Eds.), *The Oxford handbook of comparative law*, New York: Oxford University Press.

Hallin, D. C., & Mancini, P. (2004). *Comparing media systems: Three models of media and politics*. New York: Cambridge University Press.

Hibberd, M. (2005). *Il grande viaggio della BBC: Storia del servizio pubblico britannico degli anni Venti all'era digitale*. Roma: Rai-Eri.

Hitchens, L. (2006). *Broadcasting pluralism and diversity: A comparative study of policy and regulation*. Oxford: Hart Publishing.

Hoffmann-Riem, W. (1996). *Regulating media: The licensing and supervision of broadcasting in six countries*. New York: Guilford Press.

Hoskins, C., McFayden, S., & Finn, A. (2004). *Media economics: Applying economics to new and traditional media*. London: Sage.

Humphreys, P. (1996). *Mass media and media policy in Western Europe*. Manchester: Manchester University Press.

Jakubowicz, K. (2007). Public service broadcasting in 21st century: What chance for a new beginning? In G. Ferrel Lowe & J. Bardoel (Eds.), *From public service broadcasting to public service media*. Gothenburg: Nordicom.

Kelly, M. (1983). Influences on Broadcasting policies for election coverage. In J. G. Blumler (Ed.), *Communicating to voters: Television in the first European parliamentary elections*. London: Sage.

Lange, A. (2007). L'industria audiovisiva europea alla vigilia della convergenza. In C. S. Nissen (a cura di), *Fare la differenza. Il servizio pubblico radiotelevisivo nel panorama europeo*. Roma: Rai-Eri.

Lealand, G. (2008). Broadcasting and public policy: Television in New Zealand. In D. Ward (Ed.), *Television and public policy: Change and continuity in an era of global liberalization*. New York: Routledge.

Leurdijk, A. (2007). Public service media dilemmas and regulation in a converging landscape. In G. Ferrell Lowe & J. Bardoel (Eds.), *From public service broadcasting to public service media*. Gothenburg: Nordicom.

Levy, D. (1999). *Europe's digital revolution: Broadcasting revolution, the EU and the nation state*. London: Routledge.

Lijphart, A. (1971). Comparative politics and the comparative method. *American Political Science Review*, *65*, 682–693.

Luhmann, N. (2000). *The reality of the mass media*. Stanford: Stanford University Press.

Michalis, M. (2007). *Governing European communications: From unification to coordination*. Lanham: Rowman & Littlefield.

Muraro, H. (1987). La comunicación masiva durante la dictadura militar y la translación democrática en la Argentina, 1973–1986. In O. Landi (Comp.), *Medios, transformación cultural y política*. Buenos Aires: Legasa.

Pavani, G. (2016). La governance dei sistemi radiotelevisivi pubblici. Una questione culturale. *Federalismi.it. Focus Comunicazione, Media e Nuove Tecnologie*, N.1, 1–33.

Priebs, N. (2002). Learning from abroad: Regulating public service broadcasting in Germany, Japan and the UK. In J. Cowling & D. Tambini (Eds.), *From public service broadcasting to public service communications*. London: Institute for Public Policy Research.

Popper, K. R., & Condry, J. (1994). *Cattiva maestra televisione*. Roma: Donzelli.

Powe, L. A., Jr. (1987). *American broadcasting and the first amendment*. Los Angeles: University of California Press.

Reith, J. (1924). *Broadcast over Britain*. London: Hodder and Stoughton.

Sacco, R. (1992). *Introduzione al diritto comparato*. Torino: UTET.

Sartori, G. (1997). *Homo videns: Televisione e post-pensiero*. Roma-Bari: Laterza.

Scannell, P. (1989). Public service broadcasting and modern public life. *Media Culture and Society, 11*(2), 135–166.

Siebert, F. S., Peterson, T., & Schramm, W. (1956). *Four theories of the press: The authoritarian, libertarian, social responsibility, and Soviet Communist concepts of what the press should be and do*. Urbana: University of Illinois.

Simmons, S. J. (1978). *The fairness doctrine and the media*. Berkeley: University of California Press.

Terrou, F., & Solal, L. (1951). *Le droit de l'information. Etude comparée des principaux systèmes de réglementation de la presse, de la radio et du film*. Paris: Unesco.

Terzis, G. (Ed.). (2007). *European media governance: National and regional dimensions*. Chicago: The University of Chicago Press.

Tracey, M. (1998). *The decline and fall of public service broadcasting*. Oxford: Oxford University Press.

Tuchman, G. (1980). *Making news: A study in the construction of reality*. New York: Free Press.

Zack, M. G. (1970). F.C.C. and the Fairness Doctrine. *Cleveland State Law Review, 19*, 579–594.

Zeno-Zencovich, V. (2008). *Freedom of expression: A critical and comparative analysis*. Abingdon: Routledge-Cavendish.

CHAPTER 3

International and European Normative Framework

Abstract This chapter identifies the international and European law regulating the media system as well as the competent international organizations and European bodies. The aim is to guide the reader in an understanding of the supranational rules binding the member states (hard law) and those that guide their choices significantly (soft law) in the field of freedom of expression. The author identifies some common principles shared by the member states of the EU, implemented at the state level (pluralism and media independence). A prototype of Public service broadcasting that complies with these principles has now risen like a phoenix from the cultural model of the BBC, "sifted" from the ashes by the supranational organizations and based on a series of pan-European standards welcomed by national legislators.

Keywords Public service broadcasting · Media system · European law Freedom of expression · International law

Introduction

European public broadcasters are influenced by certain European standards developed by the European Union (EU) and the Council of Europe (CoE). Article 10 of the European Convention on Human Rights (ECHR) has guided the jurisprudence of the European Court of Human Rights (ECtHR) in outlining the contents of pluralism and

G. Pavani, *The Structure and Governance of Public Service Broadcasting*, https://doi.org/10.1007/978-3-319-96731-8_3

the independence of public broadcasters. The EU has no explicit competence in the media sector. Indeed, until the mid-eighties, the EU institutions remained silent on the regulation of audiovisual activities, recognizing the competence of the member states. Yet, this cultural climate gradually weakened as technological progress led to the establishment of mixed systems in all the European countries, as well as to the growing commercial importance of audiovisual activity, which required specific protections for users as well as rules to harmonize certain sections of this new market. The Court of Justice of the European Union (CJEU) classifies private and public service broadcasters as "enterprises," and as such both are subject to the EU competition and freedom of movement laws. As has often been the case in other EU contexts, economic intervention has proved to be a Trojan horse that has allowed the EU to pursue political and cultural objectives.

The International Context

Broadcasting, by its nature, knows no borders or geographical boundaries; since the introduction of satellite use, new issues in the area of international relations have emerged that cannot be resolved solely in legal terms.[1]

The existence of linguistic and cultural communities straddling national borders has made the export of broadcasts appealing (in the German-speaking area for instance or in Belgium and Luxembourg where many people speak French). The phenomenon of cross-border broadcasting has always existed, especially in Europe due to the relatively smaller size of some states. Generally, radio has created fewer problems than television broadcasting, with the exception of certain controversies surrounding the legitimacy of Soviet interventions to limit broadcasting from the West to East European Countries (a practice consistently opposed by the United Nations General Assembly, see Price 1984, p. 391).

[1] He mistrusts broadcast satellite, seeing it as "another step in a kind of information imperialism leading to substantial control, whether intentional or not, over the less developed countries through direct media access to community centers or individual homes from sources in the major developed nations" (Price 1976, p. 881). More generally, on satellite broadcasting technology, see Elbert (2008). Less up-to-date, but still a point of reference: White et al. (1996).

The international organization that took over the responsibility for regulating these aspects is the International Telecommunication Union (ITU), set up in 1856 to regulate telegraph communications and transformed in 1947 into a specialized UN institution. The ITU allocates radio-frequency spectrum and satellite orbital frequencies in compliance with a number of general principles (as outlined in UN General Assembly resolutions). These include non-discrimination in the use of satellites[2]; support, technical assistance and preferential treatment for developing Countries[3]; the orderly use of the radio-frequency spectrum and satellite orbits.[4]

The use of the regulatory instruments of international law has, therefore, been deemed necessary to avoid the "distorted" use of the radio-frequency spectrum by states, as well as to solve some problems that could not be solved at a national level.

This was particularly true when the radio-frequency spectrum was the only available platform and simultaneous broadcasting on the same frequency led to the risk of the so-called "guerre des ondes" (Debbasch 1969, p. 629 and *amplius* Part VI).

The high number of states using the airwaves and the many divergent uses (from civilian to military communications) thus necessitated international cooperation and the creation of a number of international bodies whose activities affect the broadcasting industry in different ways and to varying extents. In addition to the ITU mentioned above, there is the World Summit of the International Society (WSIS), the World Intellectual Property Organization (WIPO), the United Nations Educational Scientific and Cultural Organization (UNESCO), the Internet Corporation for Assigned Names and Numbers (ICANN) and the World Trade Organization (WTO). These global corporations and multilateral organizations, working in the light of international Treaties, "are progressively diminishing the role of individual states" on

[2]See Resolutions 1721D (XVI) of 20 December 1961 and 2915 (XXVII) of 9 December 1972.

[3]See Resolutions 1721D (XVI), cited above, and 2733 (XXV) of 16 December 1970.

[4]A principle recognized in various UIT World Radiocommunication Conferences and World Administrative Radio Conferences.

the communication policy "and new international venues are emerging to debate them" (Costanza-Chock 2005, pp. 259–275).[5]

The system of sources that together form the international regulation of broadcasting is very complex and encompasses a series of "hard" and "soft" laws, the latter being inappropriate to producing rights, but useful in enhancing uniform practices and creating common mindsets especially when it comes to sharing (and implementing) general principles. To understand the international context, we must apply criteria dealing with actual content and not what the laws nominally address and then verify each time, the type of source and the level to which they are prescriptive.

The principle of state sovereignty applies to the audiovisual sector. However, some international acts express common principles that have inspired various state laws on freedom of expression and have indirectly affected the means of communication while not directly affecting the organizational and regulatory sphere of national broadcasting systems. Of these, we should mention Article 1, para. 2 of the Constitution of UNESCO, Resolution of the General Assembly n. 59 of 14 December 1946, Article 19 of the Universal Declaration of Human Rights of 1948, whose historical precedent was Article 11 of the French Declaration of the Rights of Man and of the Citizen of 1789.

These Declarations are non-prescriptive in content, based on a common view of freedom of expression shared by participating states. Part of the internationalist scholarship accords to such Declarations the value of a recommendation or a policy text (historically see Kelsen 1950). These Declarations have then led the states to sign binding acts such as the ECHR of 1950 and the 1966 International Covenant on Civil and Political Rights. Both texts inspired other documents of more sectoral content (the Convention on the Rights of the Child, New York 1989, Article 13; the International Convention on the Elimination of All Forms of Racial Discrimination of 1965, Article 5, etc.) and created the

[5]The attempts at classification proposed by the doctrine and the international organizations themselves are hampered by the difficulties arising from the variety of objects (from radio and television to cinematography) and the scope of intervention (from the supranational to the local level, from the linguistic to the ethnic factor). They are more descriptive than prescriptive in nature and attempt to systematize the many types of organizations, bodies, specialized institutions, etc. See Linde Paniagua et al. (2009, p. 109*ff.*), which does not differ fundamentally from that of Debbasch (1969, pp. 623–645) and UNESCO's Research (1990, pp. 241–264).

theoretical basis for that neo-natural law approach that pervades the Bill of Rights adopted in many Constitutions from the 1980s onward (see Chapter 4).

The Influence of the ECHR on PSB

Article 10 ECHR represents a human rights guarantee, formulated according to the traditional concept of an individual right, granting freedom from state interference to any natural or legal person. It includes freedom to impart and receive information and ideas by using broadcasting and other electronic media.

§1 reads:

> Everyone has the right to freedom of expression. This right shall include freedom to hold opinions and to receive and impart information and ideas without interference by public authority and regardless of frontiers. This Article shall not prevent states from requiring the licensing of broadcasting, television or cinema enterprises.

The exercise of freedom of expression may be subject to licensing, but this not does affect the nature of the right stated in §1, because the ECtHR has already clarified in a judgment that a refusal to grant a licence must be judged by the conditions of Article 10§2 ECHR (*Groppera Radio AG and others v. Switzerland*, judgment of 28 March 1990, no. 10.890/84).

§2 reads:

> The exercise of these freedoms, since it carries with it duties and responsibilities, may be subject to such formalities, conditions, restrictions or penalties as are prescribed by law and are necessary in a democratic society, in the interests of national security, territorial integrity or public safety, for the prevention of disorder or crime, for the protection of health or morals, for the protection of the reputation or rights of others, for preventing the disclosure of information received in confidence, or for maintaining the authority and impartiality of the judiciary.

Article 10 ECHR, therefore, provides for general constraints linked to the occurrence of certain conditions. Thus, freedom of expression must be balanced with other rights and, where necessary, subject to restrictions. These limits have been interpreted, defined and, partly reduced over time by the ECtHR, which has acted almost as a Court of Appeal against National Courts (Barendt 1995, pp. 64–67). The Strasbourg Court has summarized the limitations on freedom of expression in the following principles: the principle of narrow interpretation; the existence of a pressing social need; proportionality and sufficient motivation.

Article 10 ECHR makes a generalized reference to the main means of communication without specifying their nature with respect to Article 34 ECHR (which only allows "non-governmental organisations" to claim to be the victim of a violation of the rights set forth in the Convention).

The ECtHR has explicitly acknowledged that public service broadcasters can be considered as "non-governmental organisations" with the right to appeal to the Court (*Radio France* and *others v. France*, judgment of 30 March 2004, no. 53.984/00; *Österreichischer Rundfunk v. Austria*, judgment of 7 December 2006, no. 35.841/02, §46 et seq. In the agreement, for example, Jarass 2005, p. 203; Grabenwarter 2012, p. 311) and it has expanded to all types of media, including PSB, the political dimension of Article 10 that was primarily attached to the press (see *inter alia*: *Jersild v. Denmark*, judgment of 23 September 1994, no. 15.890/89, §31).

So, a public service broadcaster, which is owned and/or financed by the state, may invoke Article 10, given a legal framework that guarantees editorial independence and institutional autonomy. It is the responsibility of the state to ensure its PSB is independent and free of control from political powers and to avoid it becoming subject to an all-embracing government control.

As far as the structure of PSB is concerned, "due to its subsidiary nature, the human rights protection system of the ECHR is not intended to prescribe a certain model of how broadcasting should be organised in a given country. Nevertheless, Article 10 says more about the status of public service media (PSM) than merely that a state 'may decide' to establish a public service broadcasting system, or not" (Berka and Tretter 2013, p. 3).

Initially, the ECtHR considered public monopoly as a far-reaching restriction on the freedom of expression which cannot be justified in the current European media landscape by pressing social or technical needs (*Informationsverein Lentia and others v. Austria*, judgment of 24 November 1993, no. 13.914/88). Article 10 ECHR failed to provide indications on how to avoid a monopolistic organization and did not oblige states to establish PSB or to introduce a dual broadcasting system.

The frequent decision to organize a dual broadcasting system (public–private) is the result of the state's media policy decisions and depends on the political, economic and cultural context of each country.

However, there are consequences should the state choose a "dual broadcasting system" as the Court underlined in *Manole and others v. Moldova* (judgment of 17 September 2009, no. 13.936/02, §101): "where a state does decide to create a public broadcasting system, the state is under the obligations of Article 10."

> If a state opts for a dual broadcasting system, the subsequent destruction of one of its components adversely affects the manner in which pluralism is realised in the given national situation. If a public service broadcaster was deemed necessary to provide citizens access to impartial and accurate information and a diverse range of opinion, its closure will inevitably create deficiencies. (Berka and Tretter 2013, p. 3)

In fact, the existence of PSB benefits from protection by Article 10 ECHR due to its role in a democratic society. The ECtHR has consistently highlighted the task the media must fulfil: impart information and ideas concerning matters of public interest, play the vital role of public watchdog, and serve the need for impartial, independent and balanced news, information and comment.

Hence, under Article 10§1 ECHR, states have a positive obligation to ensure pluralistic and culturally diverse media, respecting the European standards developed by the CoE and the EU with regard to the essential role and contribution of public broadcasting within a democratic society.

The EU and PSB

The European standards on PSM developed by the EU and the CoE enabled Article 10 ECHR to be linked to Article 11 of the Charter of Fundamental Rights of the European Union to interpret its significance.

Article 11 reads:

> (_1_) Everyone has the right to freedom of expression. This right shall include freedom to hold opinions and to receive and impart information and ideas without interference by public authority and regardless of frontiers.
> (_2_) The freedom and pluralism of the media shall be respected.

The initial doubts of the doctrine focused on the link to Article 10 ECHR and particularly on the applicability of Article 52§3 Charter and hence the restrictions on the freedom of expression set out in Article 10§2 ECHR[6] to Article 11 Charter, as well as the applicability of Article 52§2 Charter according to which:

> Rights recognised by this Charter for which provision is made in the Treaties shall be exercised under the conditions and within the limits defined by those Treaties.

But as previously noted, Article 11 Charter provides for a freedom on the media that "must not be understood merely as an economic freedom in the sense of the relevant provisions of the Treaty on the Functioning of the European Union (TFEU), but rather as a comprehensive right to communication that also covers PSM. The origin of this Article reveals that it is based on the freedom of expression of Article 10 ECHR though it goes further by explicitly covering freedom of the media, whose legitimacy arises from the CJEU case law on television, from the Protocol to the Treaty of Amsterdam on the system of public broadcasting in the member states, and from the "Television without Frontiers" Directive (now the Audiovisual Media Services Directive)" (Berka and Tretter 2013, p. 17).

The EU does not have any explicit competence in the media sector (*inter alias* Harrison and Woods 2007). Until the mid-eighties, the European institutions remained silent on the regulation of audiovisual activities,[7] recognizing the competence of the member states. This was mainly due to the regime of the public monopoly of PSB and the tendency to include the matter under the profile of freedom of expression,

[6] Art. 52§3 states that: "In so far as this Charter contains rights which correspond to rights guaranteed by the Convention for the Protection of Human Rights and Fundamental Freedoms, the meaning and scope of those rights shall be the same as those laid down by the said Convention. This provision shall not prevent Union law providing more extensive protection."

[7] In line with EU law, we will primarily use the term "audiovisual" (that includes the television broadcasting service), with a clarification: Directive 2010/13/EU on audiovisual media services at Recital 23 confirms the provisions of the previous Directive 2007/65/EU: "the term "audiovisual" should refer to moving images with or without sound, thus including silent films but not covering audiotransmission or radio services."

thus excluding the Community's competence in this sector (Katsirea 2008, especially part 2).

Yet, this cultural climate gradually weakened as technological progress led to the establishment of mixed systems in all the European countries, as well as to the growing commercial importance of audiovisual activity, which required specific protections for users and rules that aimed to harmonize certain sections of this new market.

The CJEU classifies private and public service broadcasters as "enterprises," both subject to the EU competition and freedom of movement laws. From its first judgment, the CJEU distinguished between the free circulation of goods and the free provision of services and included television broadcasts in this latter area. Thus, the applicability of the Treaty provisions concerning the provision of services, even to the television service (Judgment of the Court of Justice, Sacchi, Case 155/73), was ensured.

But, as has often been the case in other EU contexts, the leading path of economic intervention has proved to be a Trojan horse that has allowed the EU to pursue political and cultural objectives, so "the Commission's involvement with public broadcasting has evolved from a political to a more legalistic approach" (Donders 2012, p. 192). Not until the 1990s was the audiovisual sector included within Community competence on cultural policy (Article 151 of the TEC), although, as has been emphasized, Article 151 "does not provide the Community with powers in the area of culture but requires it to take cultural aspects into account in its action under other provisions of this Treaty" (see Castendyk et al. 2008, p. 93 and the scholarship for and against the extension of powers to cultural matters mentioned in the text).

In this sense, the audiovisual sector also extends its full potential (once again) to the cultural side, as a means of guaranteeing a fundamental right, which is the freedom of expression that the European institutions must respect as the general principle of European law, protected by the ECHR (Article 10) and the Charter of Fundamental Rights of the European Union (Article 11) (Wheeler 2010, p. 350).

There is thus a circular movement that initiates with the cultural-state dimension of the audiovisual sector, passes through the economic one (the privileged path for the entry of EU legislation) and returns to a supranational cultural dimension.

This has allowed the EU to focus on the economic value of audiovisual activities, to extend its scope and develop a European television law aimed at harmonizing the regulation of certain aspects of this service.

It should be noted, however, that the common principles formulated by the Commission have not led to the automatic harmonization of the laws of the member states nor has it imposed them a "one size fits all" approach, because "historical, social, cultural, economic and political embeddedness of public broadcasting policy is persistent even when the Commission intervenes (Donders 2012, pp. 192–193).

On the other hand, there is broad consensus on the overall "marketizing" character (Humphreys 1996, p. 174) of EU broadcasting policies; many authors have identified in the decisions of the European Commission this ongoing trend (e.g. Katsirea 2008; Harcourt 2005; Michalis 2007), that is also extending to the online versions of PSB, so "we are witnessing a process of Europeanization through marketization of the policies of PBS online" (Brevini 2013, p. 150). Anyone studying PSB online will note however that "this type of Europeanization cannot be seen as a "top-down" mechanism, where European institutions mandate the form that national policy choices should take. On the contrary, [her] study detects Europeanization as a "bottom-up" process that occurs when specific policy schemes are then transferred to the European level" (ibid., p. 150).

The path towards harmonization was started by the Commission with the 1984 Green Paper on the establishment of the Common Market for Broadcasting, especially by satellite and cable (COM (84) 300); influenced also by the European Convention on Transfrontier Television of the CoE, this led in 1989 to the Television without Frontiers Directive adopted with the heading "on the coordination of certain provisions laid down by law, regulation or administrative action in member states concerning the pursuit of television broadcasting activities," despite the initial opposition of some states.[8] After much debate between the liberal

[8]The draft directive was not welcomed by Denmark and Belgium, which challenged the competence of the Community in matters of culture, nor by Germany, where a Federal Constitutional Court's decision was required to identify the territorial level (*Bund* and *Länder*) competent for committing the will of the country in the Council (BvG 1/89, p. 57); added to this, there were protests from the United States that considered these new rules as protectionist measures that breached the GATT rules. In the vast literature, see, at least, Wallace and Goldberg (1989, p. 175*ff.*).

and dirigiste approaches, the TWF Directive was modified by Directive 97/36/EC of the European Parliament and of the Council, that integrated and clarified some of the contents that had been brought before the Court of Justice (Drijber 1999).

In the wake of the TWF Directive, the task of harmonizing the Community institutions continued: within the overall framework of a modernizing strategy called "i-2010: A European Information Society for growth and employment" (COM (2005) 229) two Directives on audiovisual media were adopted: Directive 2007/65/EU and Directive 2010/13/EU (waiting for the new Directive).[9]

So, broadcasting is qualified as a service which is protected by Article 56 TFEU which guarantees the free movement of services but can be restricted according to Article 62 in conjunction with Article 52 TFEU on justified grounds of public policy, public security or public health or with compelling reasons of public interest.

In particular, the European Courts and the Commission have always regarded PSB as a service of general economic interest which must, therefore, respect certain requirements such as: fulfilling the essential needs of citizens; ensuring access to essential services and the pursuit of priority objectives; playing a key role in social and territorial cohesion; being a prerequisite for the full exercise of fundamental rights (see COM (1996) 443 final and COM (2000) 580 final). The features listed are precisely those that have contributed to defining PSB in Europe since its beginning and that later led the EU institutions to develop a set of obligations to impose on enterprises operating a service of general economic interest (SGEI).

EU institutions have been influenced by the cultural model of Public Service Broadcasting so that at EU level also, PSB is not defined within the concept of "public television" (or, even more so, "state television") but refers to a television that fulfils the obligations of the public service.

European Standards for PSB

In the previously cited judgment *Manole and others v. Moldova* the ECtHR referred in §102 to "standards relating to public service broadcasting which have been agreed by the Contracting states through the

[9] IRIS 2017-7:1/6, European Parliament, Mandate to the Culture committee on a new directive on audiovisual media services.

Committee of Ministers of the Council of Europe" providing "guidance as to the approach which should be taken to interpreting Article 10 [ECHR] in this field" (see the informative summary by Nikoltchev 2007, pp. 7–15).

The case law of the ECtHR was inspired by various documents of the CoE (and the EU) from which the close connection between the concepts of democracy, human rights, the free circulation of information and the free expression of opinions, as well as the need for a pluralist and diverse media order, emerge clearly.

Pluralism

Among the first standards-principles established by ECtHR case law is that of pluralism,[10] supported by documents of the Committee of Ministers of the CoE such as[11]:

Recommendation n. R (97) 21 of the Committee of Ministers to member states on the media and the promotion of a culture of tolerance; Recommendation n. R (99) 1 of the Committee of Ministers to member states on measures to promote media pluralism, which invites the states to determine suitable thresholds to avoid that a single operator (or group) might influence and control the means of communication; Recommendation (2003) 9 of the Committee of Ministers to member states on measures to promote the democratic and social contribution of digital broadcasting through the strengthening of PSB; Recommendation CM/Rec (2007) 2 of the Committee of Ministers to member states on media pluralism and diversity of media content, which completes the foregoing, adapts to technological developments and invites states to pursue positive actions in favour of pluralism through the adoption of measures aimed at: promoting structural or external pluralism in the media; the promotion of diversity in content (referred to as internal pluralism); transparency in the media and the Parliamentary Assembly of the CoE such as Recommendation 2001 (n. 1506) on

[10] On the interpretation of art. 10 ECHR regarding the principle of pluralism: Oetheimer (2007). With reference to media pluralism trends in the CoE member states see the Issue Discussion Paper edited by Haraszti (2013).

[11] For a full review, see "Recommendations and Declarations of the Committee of Ministers of the Council of Europe in the field of media and information society," Strasbourg, 2016.

freedom of expression and media information, and 2003 (n. 1589), both focusing on the need to ensure a pluralistic system and independent media, considered as indispensable to the implementation of the freedom provided by Article 10 of the ECHR.

While these are legally non-binding acts, these documents have proved to be important tools for creating a common conscience on the theme of pluralism of information and its protection within the member states of the CoE.

In fact, there is no legal definition of pluralism: it has been elaborated by ECtHR case law from the more general right to impart and receive information, developed thanks to the practice of the CoE bodies and then integrated into EU law.

Since the 1980s, the ECtHR has been called upon to judge the compliance of state television regulations with the ECHR. Through its interpretation of freedom of expression, the ECtHR has verified that the principles of legality and proportionality have been respected and developed a doctrine to recognize pluralism of content, as well as (and through) the pluralism of the operators. That criterion has been repeatedly applied in the cases relating to television broadcasts (*Groppera v. Switzerland*, cited above, by which the Court states that the prohibition imposed on a Swiss company to retransmit cable and radio broadcasts from the territory of Italy is not capable of adversely affecting pluralism of content), as well as those dealing with the organizational form (*Informationsverein Lentia* and *others v. Austria*, cited above, which definitively sanctions the end of the monopolistic regime in Austria, not so much because of the organizational form itself, but because the monopoly was a disproportionate measure for the realization of content pluralism). As regards freedom of expression, the Court reiterates that it can be guaranteed only if the broadcasting systems are based on the principle of pluralism, which is ultimately safeguarded by the state (in accordance with the cases *Jersild* of 1994; *Piermont* of 1995 and *Demuth* of 2002, also dealing with compatibility with Article 10 ECHR of a prohibition by a Swiss broadcaster to re-broadcast and recently *Nenkova-Lalova v. Bulgaria*, judgment of 11 December 2012, no. 35.745/05, §57).

Within the ambiguous and multifaceted notion (Berka and Tretter 2013, p. 13) of pluralism one can distinguish between external media pluralism (structural pluralism), i.e. the existence of a diversity of independent media outlets, and pluralism of opinions (content pluralism), i.e. a variety of information and opinions diverse enough to foster an informed, uninhibited and inclusive discussion on matters of public interest.

It was earlier noted how, on the basis of the case law cited, "the pluralism of content has been reconstrued in the case law considered both as a *limit* of state power in this area (*Groppera, De Muth*), and as an *objective*, to which this power must necessarily be directed from the point of view of the Convention (*Informationsverein Lentia*)" (De Sena 2006, p. 20).

As regards case law at EU level, even the ECJ—that has increasingly referred to ECHR provisions, interpreted in the light of ECtHR case law—has already expressed regarding the "safeguarding of pluralism [which] is linked to freedom of expression, as protected by Article 10 ECHR guaranteed by Community law" (Judgment *Kabel Deutschland*, Case C-336-07).

Hence, in this area, the communicating vessels between the EU and the supranational level of the CoE are open and function effectively.

From the regulatory point of view, no specific measures were initially introduced for the protection of pluralism; rather its protection was ensured within antitrust legislation and in general measures taken to protect free competition. Since Council Directive 89/552/EEC ("Television without frontiers"), the right to impart and receive information and its corollary the principle of pluralism, have been mainly considered in aspects related to market regulation (focusing predominantly on having multiple operators, in accordance with the external profile of pluralism).

Until the Treaty of Lisbon referred to the Charter (Article 6), references were not sought in secondary law, nor treaties, but in the resolutions of the European Parliament and in the decisions provided by the ECJ.[12]

For its part, the European Parliament has complained of the lack of organic intervention in the audiovisual sector, taking into account the principle of pluralism, especially regarding the content of the broadcasts

[12] The Treaty enshrined the principle of pluralism, albeit in a wider context than that of information. Article 2 states: "The Union is founded on the values of respect for human dignity, freedom, democracy, equality, the rule of law and respect for human rights, including the rights of persons belonging to minorities. These values are common to the member states in a society in which pluralism, non-discrimination, tolerance, justice, solidarity and equality between women and men prevail."

offered. For the European Parliament, the latter is central in responding to the requirements of pluralism: diversity depends on the content of the messages and television broadcasts, and not only (although this is desirable) the number of operators present.

In Recommendation 1641 (2004) "on public service broadcasting" the Parliamentary Assembly of the CoE presents a summary of the main issues of Public Service Broadcasters in European countries, and particularly in Eastern Europe countries, where it was (is) difficult to assert independence.[13] The European Parliament also calls for respect for pluralism irrespective of nature and technique used by television companies and hopes that the climate of increasing technological convergence will not herald a convergence in the content of information and television programming.[14]

The 2010/13/EU Directive on audiovisual media services, in various Recitals, draws attention to the treaty law and the soft law tools of the EU and the aforementioned CoE and reiterates that audiovisual media services "are as much cultural services as they are economic services. Their growing importance for societies, democracy — in particular by ensuring freedom of information, diversity of opinion and media pluralism — education and culture justifies the application of specific rules to these services."

The European institutions are aware that the use of new broadcasting techniques (from satellite to Internet) may lead to an increase in the number of operators but do not automatically guarantee diversity

[13]There are also more specific Resolutions such as that addressed to the Italian Government which reports serious divergences over the years from the guidelines given by the Council of Europe (*Résolution 1387 (2004) Monopolisation des médias électroniques et possibilité d'abus de puovoir en Italie*), issued in the same year as European Parliament Resolution on the risks of violation in Europe and in particular in Italy of freedom of expression and information (2003/2237(INI)) adopted on 22 April 2004. The latest Recommendation (2012) "On public service media governance" adopted by the Committee of Ministers of the Council of Europe on 15 February 2012 is an important document providing guiding principles to adapt to the new communication environment.

[14]In the Recommendation, the Parliament "6. Stresses that the concept of the media is undergoing a redefinition through convergence, interoperability, and globalisation; considers that technological convergence and the increase in supply through internet, digital, satellite, cable and other means should not, however, result in 'convergence' of content; consumer choice and pluralism of content is the key issue, more so than pluralism of ownership or supply."

of content.[15] The phenomenon of convergence needs to be monitored to prevent it from bringing new forms of oligopoly—albeit technologically more advanced—or even monopoly of the content on offer. Convergence, together with the growing liberalization of the television market, is a new challenge for pluralism, to which not only the member states but also to the EU overall, must respond.

This, in part, has been accomplished in recent years. Even within the limits of the competences already highlighted, the EU has also had an impact on national legislation on pluralism and on regulating a sector, or rather a fragment of the wider communications sector, namely that of electronic communications.

The 2002 EC Directives package addressed the world of communications as a whole. Indeed, precisely in the light of the phenomenon of convergence, telecommunications and radio and television networks and services were made subject to the same regulatory framework. In this context, EU legislature intervened in areas where it already exercised its powers, dictating rules on important aspects, such as consumer protection, access to networks and services, protection of personal data, cultural diversity and so on, to ensure unified regulation of the services regardless of the technology used (Nihoul and Rodford 2004).[16] Although this unified regulatory framework was not drafted for the explicit protection of pluralism, it does show a favourable approach to certain issues closely related to this principle, such as the focus on the cultural and linguistic diversity.

In the context of new media services,[17] the participation of PSB is seen as increasingly important by the European institutions (see

[15] In the Recommendation, the Parliament "7. Notes that digital media will not automatically guarantee greater choice, because the same media companies that already dominate the national and global media markets also control the dominant content portals on the Internet, and since the promotion of digital and technical literacy are strategic issues for the development of lasting media pluralism, and expresses concern about the switching off of the analogue frequencies in some parts of the Union."

[16] With reference to the following Directives: n. 2002/21/EC (Framework Directive); n. 2002/20/EC (Authorization Directive); n. 2002/19/EC (Access Directive); n. 2002/22/EC (Universal Service Directive). In addition, Directive 2002/77/EC on competition in the markets of audiovisual networks and services.

[17] Various Recommendations of the Committee of Ministers and the Parliamentary Assembly of the CoE refer to the new media ecosystem, which should encompass all actors and factors whose interaction allows the media to function and to fulfil their role in society (Recommendation Rec (2011) 7 on a new notion of media).

Recommendation CM/Rec 3 (2007) of the Committee of Ministers to member states on the remit of PSM in the information society). The European Parliament refers to broadcast media as one of the most important sources of information available to citizens, and as such, an important factor in shaping people's values and opinions (European Parliament Resolution of 25 November 2010 on public service broadcasting in the digital era: the future of the dual system (2010/2028(INI)), Recital B); "both public service and private-sector broadcasting have a crucial role to play with regard to European audiovisual production, cultural diversity and identity, information, pluralism, social cohesion, the promotion of fundamental freedoms and the functioning of democracy" (European Parliament Resolution of 25 November 2010 on public service broadcasting in the digital era: the future of the dual system (2010/2028(INI)) Recital C).

Independence and Funding of PSB

Closely linked to pluralism is the standard-principle of independence (Comparative Report of the European Commission, Media freedom and independence in 14 European countries: A comparative perspective, July 2012), which should guide the choices of states on governance; see: the Recommendation CM/Rec (2012) 1 of the Committee of Ministers to Member States on public service media governance, adopted on 15 February 2012, implemented by the Recommendation and Resolution on political influence over independent media and journalists, adopted by the Parliamentary Assembly of the Council of Europe (PACE) on 29 June 2017, quality of programming (See the European Parliament Resolution of 25 November 2010 on "public service broadcasting in the digital era: the future of the dual system" (2010/2028(INI)) and financing to support their public service broadcasters).

Among the Council's Documents highlighting the importance of the independence of PSB organizations in democratic societies, we note the Declaration of the Committee of Ministers on the guarantee of the independence of public service broadcasting in the member states (adopted by the Committee of Ministers on 27 September 2006 at the 974th meeting of the Ministers' Deputies) that recalls Recommendation n. R (96) 10 on "The Guarantee of the Independence of Public Service Broadcasting" (1996) with which the Committee of Ministers adopted a number of detailed guidelines aimed at ensuring the independence of

PSB (including the rules governing the status and appointment of the members of the boards of management and the supervisory bodies of PSB [that] "should be defined in a way which avoids any risk of political or other interference").

The funding method of public broadcasters is among the criteria used to test their independence as it reflects the relations between state, society, culture and market in a country.

The pursuit of tasks assigned to public broadcasters requires support from state institutions (and/or regional ones, depending on the degree of decentralization), as both the Constitutional Courts of many countries and the European Courts have repeatedly stated. At the same time, the considerable costs of creating a television service often require(d) the use of private funding. The balance between the two modes falls within the criteria for assessing the independence of public broadcasters from political power, on the one hand, and the yoke of large commercial enterprises on the other (Recommendation n. R (96) 10, cit. the funding envisaged should not be used to "exert, directly or indirectly, any influence over the editorial independence and institutional autonomy" of PSB; moreover, financing must be adopted in a "long-term" perspective so as to guarantee "the continuity of the activities.").

Even when the funding of public broadcasters is not the principal focus, CoE Recommendations do not overlook the fact that funding affects the independence of PSB and its technological development (Recommendation Rec (2003) 9 and Recommendation CM/Rec (2007) 3).

After the collapse of the broadcasting monopolies, many European countries established a mixed funding model for PSB that combines different types of resources coming from two major categories: licence fees and other forms of public funding, and private sources (such as split screen, virtual advertising and interactive advertising; see Chapter 5).

The European Court of Justice has reinserted public funding for PSB within the category of state aid, and in its first judgments considered them compatible with the common market (Case NN 141/95, Financing of public Portuguese television), removing the label of the "ugly duckling" of competition law from state aid control or EU state aid policy (Donders 2012, p. 61; Grespan and Bellodi 2006, p. 327; Pesaresi and Van Hoof 2008, Ch. 1).

EU competence (and interference) translates into the ability to monitor the application of the state aid rules contained in Articles 107(1) and

106(2) of the TFEU (Jurgen Sacker and Montag 2016). It is the responsibility of the Commission to monitor "the application of the provisions [...] by addressing, where appropriate, the member states' appropriate guidelines or decisions."[18]

On the assumption that "generally [...] state funding of public broadcasters may also affect trade between member states," the Commission referred to the landmark judgment in Altmark (Case C-280/00) of the European Court of Justice to restate the four criteria laid down for public service compensation to be free of state aid elements.

Conclusion

In this chapter, I have sought to demonstrate how the EU has acquired competence in the broadcasting sector, through a circular movement that initiates with the cultural dimension of the audiovisual sector at a state level, passes through the economic sphere (the privileged path for the entry of EU legislation) and returns to a supranational, cultural dimension. This has allowed the EU to focus on the economic value of audiovisual activities, to extend its scope and develop a European television law aimed at harmonizing the regulation of certain aspects of this service.

European institutions have repeatedly reaffirmed the relevance of PSB in the new digital era and the importance for PSB to develop online media services, also underlining support for the expansion of PSB into the online world.

The CoE and the European Commission, though using different tools and with different purposes, both tend to reinforce the importance of PSB and urge the states to adopt regulations that are homogeneous (to the extent possible) and comply with the principles of pluralism and media independence.

Regarding mission and remits, a prototype of PSB that complies with these principles has now risen like a phoenix from the cultural model of the BBC, "sifted" from the ashes by the supranational organizations and based on a series of pan-European standards welcomed by national legislators.

[18]Art. 106(3). The case of the *Netherlands v. Commission* (T-231/06 r T-237/06), deals with the relationship between Art. 107 TFEU (prohibition of state aid) and Art. 106, para. 2 TFEU (exemption from the prohibition for public service reasons).

References

Barendt, E. (1995). *Broadcasting law: A comparative study*. Oxford: Oxford University Press.

Berka, W., & Tretter, H. (2013). *Public service media under article 10 of the European convention on human rights*. Geneve: European Broadcasting Union.

Brevini, B. (2013). *Public service broadcasting online: A comparative European policy study of PSB 2.0*. London: Palgrave Macmillan.

Castendyk, O., Dommering, E., Scheuer, A., & Böttcher, K. (Eds.). (2008). *European media law*. Austin: Kluwer Law International.

Costanza-Chock, S. (2005). The globalization of media policy. In R. McChesney, R. Newman, & B. Scott (Eds.), *The future of media: Resistance and reform in the 21st century*. New York, London, Toronto, and Melbourne: Seven Stories Press.

Debbasch, C. (1969). *Le droit de la radio et de la télévision*. Paris: PUF.

De Sena, P. (2006). Convenzione europea dei diritti dell'uomo e legge Gasparri: alcune riflessioni su pluralismo e televisione digitale. In R. Mastroianni (a cura di), *Il sistema radiotelevisivo e la legalità europea*. Napoli: ESI.

Donders, K. (2012). *Public service media and policy in Europe*. New York: Palgrave Macmillan.

Drijber, B. J. (1999). The revised television without frontiers directive: Is it fit for the next century? *Common Market Law Review, 36*, 87–122.

Elbert, B. R. (2008). *Introduction to satellite communication* (3rd ed.). Norwood, MA: Artech House.

Grabenwarter, P. (2012). *Europäische Menschenrechtskonvention* (5th ed.). München: C.H. Beck.

Grespan, D., & Bellodi, L. (2006). State aid. In G. L. Tosato & L. Bellodi (Eds.), *EU Competition Law—Volume I: Procedure anti-trust, merger, state aid*. Brussels: Claeys Casteel.

Haraszti, M. (Ed.). (2013). *Media pluralism and human rights*. Commissioner for Human Rights and prepared by, available under https://wcd.coe.int/ViewDoc.jsp?id=1881589.

Harcourt, A. (2005). *The European Union and the regulation of media markets*. Manchester: Manchester University Press.

Harrison, J., & Woods, L. M. (2007). *European broadcasting law and policy*. Cambridge: Cambridge University press.

Humphreys, P. (1996). *Mass media and media policy in Western Europe*. Manchester: Manchester University Press.

Jarass, H. D. (2005). *EU-Grundrechte*. München: C. H. Beck.

Jurgen Sacker, F., & Montag, F. (Ed.). (2016). *European state aid law: A commentary*. Oxford: C.H. Beck.

Katsirea, I. (2008). *Public broadcasting and European law: A comparative examination of public service obligations in six member states.* Austin: Kluwer Law International.

Kelsen, H. (1950). *The law of the United Nations: A critical analysis of its fundamental problems.* New York: Praeger.

Linde Paniagua, E., Vidal Beltrán, J. M., & Medina González, S. (2009). *Derecho audiovisual* (3rd ed.). Madrid: Colex.

Michalis, M. (2007). *Governing European communications.* Lanham, MD: Lexington.

Nihoul, P., & Rodford, P. (2004). *EU electronic communications law: Competition and regulation in the European telecommunications market.* Oxford: Oxford University Press.

Nikoltchev, S. (2007). European backing for public service broadcasting, Council of Europe rules and standards. In Iris Special, *The public service broadcasting culture.* Strasbourg: European Audiovisual Observatory.

Oetheimer, M. (2007). *Freedom of expression in Europe: Case-law concerning article 10 of the European convention on human rights.* Strasbourg: Council of Europe Publishing.

Pesaresi, N., & Van Hoof, M. (2008). Chapter 1: State aid control: An introduction. In W. Mederer, N. Pesaresi, & M. Van Hoof (Eds.), *EC competition law: Volume IV, state aid.* Brussels: Claeys Casteel.

Price, M. E. (1976). The first amendment and television broadcasting by satellite. *UCLA Law Review, 23*, 879–903.

Price, R. B. (1984). Jamming and the law of international communications. *Michigan Yearbook of International Legal Studies 5*, 391–403.

UNESCO's Research. (1990). *World communication report.* Paris.

Wallace, R., & Goldberg, D. (1989). The EEC directive on television broadcasting. *Yearbook of European Law, 9*(1), 175–196.

Wheeler, M. (2010). The EU's competition directorate: State aids and public service broadcasting. In P. Iosifidis (Ed.), *Reinventing public service communication: European broadcasters and beyond.* New York: Palgrave Macmillan.

White, S., Bate, S., & Johnson, T. (1996). *Satellite communications in Europe: Law and regulation* (2nd ed.). London: FT Law & Tax.

CHAPTER 4

Constitutional Context and Legal Framework

Abstract This chapter considers the constitutional texts that contain an explicit reference to television, particularly Public service broadcasting. The author also analyses what she calls the "silent legal systems", namely those whose constitutions contain no statements on television, but whose broadcasting systems have nevertheless developed through the jurisprudence of constitutional courts (e.g. the judicial construction of a right, as in the case of *Rundfunkfreiheit* in Germany). In some cases, the para-legislative role of the Constitutional Courts has compensated for a slow legislator that devoted little attention to the development of the media (e.g. Italy). The constitutional landscape described in this chapter enables the reader to place PSB in a specific (constitutional) context and highlights certain rules that have frequently resulted from judgments in the Constitutional Courts.

Keywords Public service broadcasting · Television · Constitution
Constitutional courts · *Rundfunkfreiheit*

Introduction

Like the form of state, the catalogue of rights contained in a Constitution reflect each nation's legal and cultural traditions and enable us to identify the elements that differentiate countries belonging to the liberal-democratic model—for which the media contribute to the full

G. Pavani, *The Structure and Governance of Public Service Broadcasting*, https://doi.org/10.1007/978-3-319-96731-8_4

expression of thought and the free formation of public opinion—and those lying outside this model. For the latter, broadcasting may pursue different goals such as the spread of Islamic culture (thought expressed *on* radio and *on* TV must be guaranteed, but provided it is "in accordance with the Islamic criteria and the best interests of the country": Article 175 Constitution of Iran), or be used for the "exclusive service of the working people and in the interests of society" (Article 53 Constitution of Cuba) and "of socialism" (Article 22 Constitution of China). Research conducted on all the constitutional texts, with no temporal, geographical or legal-cultural limits, clearly shows that few constitutions contain a reference to broadcasting, even in those non-EU countries that have adopted or deeply revised their constitutional texts in the last 15–20 years (Pavani 2012, pp. 21–43).

In this chapter, I will consider the constitutional texts that contain an explicit reference to television, particularly PSB, including the titles and/or chapters of the new Constitutions that deal with communication and new media. I will also analyse what I would call the "silent legal systems," namely those whose Constitutions contain no statements on television, but whose broadcasting systems have nevertheless developed through the jurisprudence of Constitutional Courts (e.g. the case of *Rundfunkfreiheit* in Germany). In some cases, the para-legislative role of the Constitutional Courts has compensated for a slow, or sometimes inactive, legislator that devoted little attention to the development of the media (e.g. Italy). I will demostrate "the constitutional dimension" of the public service broadcasting (Vigevani 2017, p. 1*ff.*).

The Constitutional Context

In many recent Constitutions outside Europe, the "Bill of Rights" is inspired by theories that evoke a return to "international" natural law and involve the drafting of articles that are closely copied from the International Declaration of Human Rights.

Generally, broadcasting appears in the article dealing with the freedom of expression, as one of the instruments for the spreading of thought, similarly to the telephone or telegraph.[1] However, the potential of

[1] The text that follows (Art. 20, para. 2 Constitution of Barbados) is identical to Arts. 79, para. 2 Constitution of Kenya; 14, para. 2 Constitution of Lesotho; 25, para. 2 Constitution of Sierra Leone; 23, para. 2 Constitution of Bahamas; 20, para. 2 Constitution of Barbados; 12, para. 2 Constitution of Belize; 46, para. 2 Constitution of

broadcasting is more relevant in those Constitutions that entrust it with particular purposes: for example, it is at the service of the state to spread and teach the Constitution and the main International Declaration of Human Rights (Article 40 Constitution of Benin), or to contribute to the implementation of the right to education alongside various social actors ranging from the family to the state (Article 63 Constitution of the Dominican Republic), as well as to the forming of public opinion and the strengthening of various cultural aspects (from national identity to the protection of the culture amd languages of ethnic minorities). There are few Consitutions that dedicate entire sections to "information and communication," such as that of Ecuador (2009).

In Europe, the Constitutions adopted between the liberal period and the mid-1970s, refer solely to the press that dominated communications at the time, and the radio that in the first half of the twentieth century was used primarily for propaganda and then for providing information during the World Wars.

Despite many constitutional amendments, generally the "Bill of Rights" of these Constitutions was left unchanged and was not updated to include the new aspects of certain freedoms (such as the freedom to receive and impart information), and especially not the media. The coupling "freedom of expression-freedom of press" remains valid in the European liberal Constitutions that have generally failed to add articles dedicated to the media (and even less to the new media). The exception is Switzerland, that in its completely revised Constitution of 2000 regulates certain means of communication that could not be contemplated in that of 1874[2] and

Guyana and only varies Art. 12, para. 3 Constitution of Antigua and Barbuda: "Nothing contained in or done under the authority of any law shall be held to be inconsistent with or in contravention of this section to the extent that the law in question makes provision [...] b. that is reasonably required for the purpose of protecting the reputations, rights and freedoms of other persons or the private lives of persons concerned in legal proceedings, preventing the disclosure of information received in confidence, maintaining the authority and independence of the courts or regulating the administration or technical operation of telephony, telegraphy, posts, wireless broadcasting, television or other means of communication or regulating public exhibitions or public entertainments; [...]."

[2]Art. 93, included in the part of the Constitution dealing with the competences of the Confederation, the Cantons and the Municipalities, attributes legislation on broadcasting to the Confederation (para. 1), and lays down the key principles and values in this area, starting with the definition of the broadcasting mission, pluralism of information (para. 2), medium independence and autonomy of the programmes (para. 3).

includes an article on "freedom *of the* media" (Article 17) that is separate from that on freedom of expression (Article 16).

Some of the Constitutions drafted after the Second World War do not even mention the radio, such as the Italian Constitution (Article 21) or the French Constitution for reasons of structure (the fundamental rights are contained in the preamble and freedom of expression is protected in Arts. 10 and 11 of the *Déclaration des Droits de l'Homme et du Citoyen* of 1789). Article 5 of the Basic Law for the Federal Republic of Germany differs slightly as it recognizes the "rights of communication," including the *Rundfunkfreiheit* (freedom of broadcasting), as indicated in the interpretation of the Constitutional Court.

Where the Constitution contains no provisions, nor even a mention, related to broadcasting, it has been necessary to implement an extensive interpretation of the norms concerning the freedom of expression. In this sense, scholarship and jurisprudence, especially of a constitutional nature, have played a crucial role by guiding the legislator in the implementation of the constitutional texts.

All too often, however, especially during the earlier periods of broadcasting, an extensive interpretation struggled to gain acceptance, being hampered by legal theory that was reluctant to apply the constitutional guarantees recognized to the press to the new means of communication by analogy. This approach in the theory affected the early Liberal Constitutions of the Scandinavian countries, which were revised or replaced by texts whose references to fundamental freedoms remain largely faithful to the nineteenth century formulation. With the exception of Sweden,[3] these Constitutions are characterized by the absence of any reference to broadcasting and a mere recognition of the freedom of expression. For example, the wording of Article 77 of the Danish Constitution of 1953 is identical to the previous one of 1849. Sometimes freedom of expression has been added with a twofold, active and passive profile, as with the latest Finnish Constitution of 2000 (Article 12). Following a constitutional reform in Norway, a break was made in the coupling of freedom of expression with freedom of press,

[3]The revised 1975 Constitution opens to the new media: Chapter 2, Art. 1 of the Law on the Instrument of Government of 1989 mentions broadcasting, and the subsequent Basic Law on Freedom of Expression of 1991 extends the regulation of radio programming to television.

and only the former is regulated along with right to receive and impart information.[4]

Of the Constitutions drafted in the mid-1970s, Spain briefly mentions broadcasting in the article dealing with the division of legislative powers between the state and the *Comunidades Autónomas*, which entrusts the state with the basic regulation of the press, radio and television and the *Comunidades Autónomas* (Article 149.1, No. 27) with developing such regulation, while the Constitutions of Greece in 1975 and Portugal in 1976 devote greater space to the regulation of broadcasting.

The parts of the Eastern European Constitutions drafted in the 1990s that are devoted to fundamental freedoms recall the approach of those of Western Europe while almost universally integrating the principles of the ECHR, which hovered over the constitutional-drafting processes of the period. There are few articles on broadcasting; the legislators-constitutional reviewers of the new democracies of the East, failed to take this opportunity to constitutionalize the most widespread media of the time.[5]

In the few cases where broadcasting is mentioned in the Constitution, it is considered to be a tool not only for implementing civil liberties but also political participation rights. The aspects most commonly regulated (usually by the ordinary legislator) are access and use of broadcasting during election campaigns.

In these cases, broadcasting is not only one of the possible ways of exercising freedom of expression, but becomes the prerequisite for the existence of certain subjective legal situations, as well as an indispensable tool for its implementation.

Thus, constitutional value was granted to rights generally governed by legislation on the electoral system, such as the "Right of broadcasting time," namely the right to a time slot in public broadcasts on radio

[4]Norway changed the 1814 Constitution by adding new rights, specifically the right to receive and impart information, thus amending Art. 100 which only contemplated the above-mentioned coupling. On the revision of Art. 100, preceded by a Green Paper (Stortingsmelding) in 2004, see Rieber-Mohn (2004).

[5]The classical freedom to express thoughts in word, in writing, and with "every other means of communication," extends almost everywhere to include the freedom to receive and disseminate information (Latvia, Art. 100, Estonia, Arts. 44 and 45, Slovenia, Art. 39, para. 1); sometimes the articles also contain the guaranteed prohibition of censorship of mass media, especially by the state, political parties and public organizations (Lithuania, Art. 44).

and television granted to specific categories (especially political parties) during certain periods (electoral campaigns)[6]; or the "Right of reply" (Article 40 Constitution of Portugal and Article 31.5 Constitution of Romania), sometimes referred to as Right of reply and political argument (Article 14.5 Constitution of Greece).[7]

Some Constitutions also regulate the organizational profile and the rules on access with an authorisation permit (a purposely generic term to indicate any form of act issued by a public entity to allow broadcasting), in implementation of Article 10 ECHR (Article 19.5 of the Constitution of Cyprus, Article 14.9 of the Constitution of Greece, Article 54 of the Constitution of Poland, Article 26 of the Slovak Republic). In some cases there are constraints on media ownership, particularly electronic media, to avoid concentration (Article 14.9 Constitution of Greece) and the specific "social mission" of the tool of broadcasting in order to differentiate it from the press (Greece, Arts. 14.9 and 15.2 respectively).

There are a number of Constitutions that go beyond merely mentioning broadcasting, by expressly indicating the form of organization of the public service broadcasting and thus recognizing the European model (Article 122 Constitution of Cyprus; Article 38.5 Constitution of Portugal). In these cases, the PSB is entrusted with the task of enhancing both national and European identity, strengthening ethnic minorities and protecting the needs of religious communities, and so on (Article 61.4,

[6] In Portugal, the "direito, nos termos da lei, a tempos de antena no serviço público de rádio e televisão, a ratear de acordo com a sua representatividade," which was attributed to a series of organizations whose level of representativeness is established by law (trade unions, political parties, professional organizations, organizations representing economic activities and other social organizations), becomes "direito a tempos de antena, regulares e equitativos, nas estações emissoras de rádio e de televisão de âmbito nacional e regional" during election periods (Art. 40, entitled "Direitos de antena, de resposta e de réplica política," amended in 1982, 1989, 1997 and in 2004). Art. 31, para. 5 of the Romanian Constitution strictly links it to Public radio and television services, which "must guarantee any important social and political group the exercise of the right to broadcasting time [...]."

[7] "Every person offended by an inaccurate publication or broadcast has the right to reply, and the information medium has a corresponding obligation for full and immediate redress. Every person offended by an insulting or defamatory publication or broadcast has also the right to reply, and the information medium has a corresponding obligation to immediately publish or transmit the reply. The manner in which the right to reply is exercised and in which full and immediate redress is assured or publication and transmission of the reply is made, shall be specified by law."

Constitution of Hungary, in the text adopted with the constitutional review of 2010, which remained in force until 31 December 2011).

Most of the Constitutions that regulate the organizational profile of broadcasting companies also establish an independent authority responsible for the supervision and regulation of the communications sector: Article 15 Constitution of Greece; Arts. 118–119 Constitution of Malta, amended in 1974; Arts 213–215 Constitution of Poland; Article 39 Constitution of Portugal; Article 61 Constitution of Hungary.

Usually, the Constitutions merely sketch the structure of these Authorities, leaving the rules on its composition, operation and functions to be laid down by law. In some cases, however, they also set out the procedures for the selection of members—that almost always involve Parliament—to further safeguard the indispensable requirement of their independence (Article 118 of the Constitution of Malta, Article 61.4 Constitution of Hungary).

The Creative (and Surrogate) Role of the Constitutional Courts

Constitutional and Supreme Courts have played a significant role in building a "freedom of broadcasting", by contributing to the adaptation of the text to the (new) constitutional context and by setting out some of the regulatory models that have spread beyond state boundaries.

The Courts have laid down the constitutional principles to which legislators referred when creating broadcasting legislation, especially when it goes unmentioned in Constitutions.

The first example of this commitment comes from the United States: the oldest Constitution in the world to contemplate freedom of expression, in conjunction with that of the press (according to the First Amendment). This association ensured that the press would also enjoy the guarantees of freedom of expression (axiom confirmed in *Gitlow v. New York*, 268 US 666, 1925) and that liberal US legal thought dealt widely with this medium, so the rights of the individual are guaranteed with minimal state intervention.

The regulation of broadcasting media therefore created an obvious exception to the principles of liberalism expressed in that constitutional norm, and required a complex theoretical construction capable of justifying state intervention (Chapter 2). A constitutional provision couched in negative terms ("Congress shall make no law [...] abridging the freedom *of speech, or of the press*"), which regulates only the active profile of freedom of expression and contemplates only one instrument beyond words, has inspired the guiding principles for the discipline of other media for which the First Amendment—identical in its initial formulation, but with further content added—remains the guiding star.

This task was mainly carried out by the Supreme Court which interpreted the synthetic Bill of Rights to extend the guarantees of First Amendment to other media (onwards from *Freedman v. Maryland*, 380 U.S. 51, 57 (1965)).

In Europe too, Constitutional Courts have made a significant and original contribution to the interpretation of the Constitutional texts, as the two selected cases of Germany and Italy show. However, the initial choice has been an organizational model opposed to that of the United States.

Germany. The Jurisprudential Construction of the *Rundfunkfreiheit*

Unlike other Constitutions of the second half of the 1940s, the 1949 Basic Law (*Grundgesetz*—GG) is innovative because it recognizes the right to receive and impart information and mentions the radio among the means of implementing freedom of expression. Article 5.1 GG establishes that: "Every person shall have the right freely to express and disseminate his opinions in speech, writing and pictures, and to inform himself without hindrance from generally accessible sources. Freedom of the press and freedom of reporting by means of broadcasts and films shall be guaranteed". In addition to the freedom of expression and the right to receive and impart information, the GG therefore recognizes the so-called rights of communication, namely freedom of the press, cinema and, literally, the freedom of information *through* the radio ("die Freiheit der Berichterstattung *durch* Rundfunk").

This provides the essential source, as the Constitutional Court has stated (BverfGE, 12, 205 (261)).

Although Article 5 does not explicitly sanction a freedom of broadcasting in parallel with the (recognized) freedom of the press, it is not possible to reduce the provision under consideration to a mere guarantee of the freedom to report the news through the radio (see at least von Mangoldt et al. 1999, Article 5 I, II para. 100). This decision uses the term *Rundfunk*, which corresponds to the word radio, but as a careful (Spanish) legal scholar emphasized, "in the Constitution [*Rundfunk* is] a super concept that includes radio (*Hörfunk*) and television (*Fernsehfunk*), as the German Constitutional Court stated since its first judgments" (González Encinar 1996, p. 64).

The television system has been formed through a thorough interpretation by the Constitutional Court, which "behaves as the main actor in the media scene"[8] and has made the "German model" a point of reference in Europe for the way in which pluralism is guaranteed through the regulation of the media (González Encinar 2000, p. 97; Klotz 2000, pp. 123–137. Recently: Arenas Ramiro 2015, p. 539*ff.*).

In the series of rulings handed down by the Constitutional Court, the second and third theses of the Freedom of Speech (self-fulfilment e participation in democracy)[9] have prevailed and the doctrine of the dual content of fundamental rights was adopted: an objective and a subjective one.[10]

The so-called broacasting judgments[11] have therefore shaped the *Rundfunkfreiheit*, namely the "freedom of television" (BverfGE7, 198, (205)) with the following characteristics.

[8] Hoffmann-Riem and Schulz 1996, p. 64 and, in greater detail, Hoffmann-Riem (1994, p. 17*ff.*). On the role of the Constitutional Court in defining the content of freedom of expression, see Zimmermann (2011 p. 145*ff.*).

[9] The four theoretical models, emerging from interpretations in the literature and jurisprudence, coming especially from US case law and used to justify the Free Speech Principle, and the special protection it is given, are well explained in Barendt (2005, pp. 6–23) ("(i) Arguments concerned with the importance of discovering truth"; "(ii) Free speech as an aspect of self-fulfilment"; "(iii) The argument from citizen participation in a democracy"; "(iv) Suspicion of government.").

[10] Stern distinguishes two additional elements within the objective content: the objective legal content and institutional guarantees. This distinction is particularly important for understanding the different contents of television freedom Stern (1994). On the positions of doctrine, see in brief Engelke (1992, p. 19*ff.*).

[11] The judgments are: 1st, of 28 February 1961 (BVerfGE 12, 205); 2nd, of 27 July 1971 (BVerfGE 31, 314); 3rd, of 16 June 1981 (BVerfGE 57, 295); 4th, of 4 November 1986 (BVerfGE 73, 118); 5th, of 24 March 1987 (BVerfGE 74, 297); 6th, of 5 February 1991 (BVerfGE 83, 238); 7th, of 6 October 1992 (BVerfGE 87, 181); 8th, of 22 February 1994 (BVerfGE 90, 60); 9th, of 22 February 1995 (BVerfGE 92, 203); 10th, of 17 February 1998 (BVerfGE 97, 228); 11th, of 20 February 1998 (BVerfGE 97, 298); 12th, of 11 September 2007 (BVerfGE 119, 181); 13th, of 12 March 2008 (BVerfGE 121, 30); and the 14th, of 25 March 2014 (1 BvF 1/11).

The Constitutional Court has adopted an intermediate position between the legal theory that considers *Rundfunkfreiheit* as a special form of freedom of expression (through a specific means of communication: Hoffmann-Riem, 1994), and that considering it as a fundamental freedom with autonomous content, constructed through successive case law (Bullinger 1989, p. 667*ff.*). The Constitutional Court, with a functionalist interpretation, qualified the freedom of television as "serving freedom" (*Dienende Freiheit*): its function is to contribute to the formation (and protection) of free public and individual opinion, hence—and this is the fundamental passage for its interpretation—it is the function itself that determines and influences the structure and the content of the basic right (BverfGE, 57, 297, 319).

The Constitutional Court defined television as a "special" medium of communication both for the steep costs and complex technology initially needed for television broadcasting and the persuasive power that television (understood as the "medium" and "factor"), exercises in the formation of public opinion: BverfGE, 12, 205 (261) and BverfGE, 57, 295 (322–323). On the basis of this specificity, the Constitutional Court ruled that the function would be implemented with the provision of essential television services (*Grundversorgung*), which in German legal theory do not coincide with the concept of traditional public services. Although the concept of public services is not homogeneous in all legal systems, here the reference is to the *traditional* concept that many European countries (including Germany) have inherited from the French administrative tradition and which they also use in the context of public service broadcasting. German jurisprudence (supported by the theory) did not use this category. The explanation should be sought in the structure of freedom of broadcasting which is a freedom from the state, so "there is no freedom of television if the state provides the public service". For this reason, the category of public service has been rejected in favour of the "Grundversorgung", which is already in use in German public law for certain social security rights (BverfGE, 74, 297 (326)) and has been adapted to TV.

If public television is to fulfill the purposes of an essential service, it must not only inform, entertain and contribute to the formation of a public opinion, but will also have a cultural responsibility (BVerfGE 73, 118).

These features affect the two contents of the freedom of broadcasting.

The subjective content consists of a right of defence against the state. Protection to television broadcasting is afforded against any influence of public powers and, in particular, of the political majority of Parliament and government (BverfGE, 12, 205 (260) onwards). It is not therefore a traditional subjective right to defend an individual against the state because this freedom protects television broadcasting to the extent that it contributes to fulfilling its fundamental function of forming free public opinion. The creation of television is excluded from the subjective scope, since the Constitutional Court did not consider it closely related to the function (BverfGE, 57, 295 (318)).

The objective content implies precise obligations vis-à-vis public authorities and is split into two further elements: the objective legal content (formed by the principle outlined in the rules on fundamental rights) and the institutional guarantee (against the legislator, who is asked to regulate and organize certain public institutions, within its mandate). The principle that integrates the objective legal content is the freedom of television from politics (*Staatsfreiheit des Rundfunks*), which obliges all public authorities to promote and protect it. In order to fulfill this obligation, and thus to make the freedom of television effective, the legislator (or rather, the *Länder*, that are the governing bodies responsible) implements it by adopting regulations on the organization of the broadcasting regime (Starck 1973, p. 5*ff.*). The function protected by law (the formation of public opinion) requires an active engagement primarily by the legislator who is responsible for giving substance to that abstract concept of *Ausgestaltung* which, according to scholars, also applies to the legal regime of broadcasting. Translated into simpler terms, and borrowing our terminology from a well-known classification of rights, we are not dealing with a negative freedom, but a positive freedom. Hence, it is not enough for the legislator to abstain in order to form an area of such freedom, but rather concrete interventions (*eine positive Ordnung*) are needed, especially to regulate the organization. In other words, the concept of *Ausgestaltung* does not apply to restrictions on the substantive freedom of television aimed at the protection of individual subjective situations (such as privacy or the rights of minors), for which the law provides specific safeguards.

The Constitutional Court, however, merely set the framework for freedom: it did not provide a precise model of television, but left such a choice to the legislator (who initially, as happened in other states, opted for a monopoly of public corporation broadcasting before switching to a mixed model). In fulfilling this mandate, the legislator resorted to a well-known form of organization in German administrative law: the institution of public law which on this occasion, became the institution of public law for public service broadcasters (*öffentlich-rechtliche Rundfunkanstalten*), later joined by private TVs (Arnold 1997, p. 381).

German Influence on Spanish Law

The Court of Karlsruhe's case-law on the freedom of television has been closely studied by Spanish legal scholars, particularly from the school of Professor Juan G. Encinar of the University of Alcalá de Henares. The dual content theory of fundamental rights has been transposed both by the Constitutional Court (since judgment 25/1981) and by Spanish legal theory.[12]

The approach of the German Constitutional Court has profoundly inspired its Spanish counterpart, in particular in two passages: freedom of expression is a fundamental right, but it is also a guarantee for the formation of free opinion, thus the legislator must intervene to regulate the possible entry of private corporations into the broadcasting system.[13]

The foremost case is judgment STC 12/1982 of March 31, better known as the "Sentencia Antena TV", adopted shortly after the approval of the basic law on the broadcasting system (*Lei* 4/1980, "Estatuto de la Radio y la Televisión." in force, with amendments, until *Lei* 7/2010 on audiovisual communication), which emphasizes the nature of the essential public service of television, within the terms of Article 128, para. 2 of the Constitution.

The Constitutional Court begins with a reflection on freedom of expression (regulated by Article 20 of the Constitution) deeply

[12] For a philosophical perspective, see the seminal Peces-Barba Martínez (1999). On the influence of German case law in Spain, see, at least, Bastida Freijedo (1998, p. 351*ff.*).

[13] For the reconstruction of *Rundfunkfreiheit* through Spanish-language studies, a text whose basic thesis remains valid is that of Salvador Martínez (1998) where the method of analysis is based on faithful reconstruction of case law made by the Constitutional Court, alongside the analytical proposal put forward by Klaus Stern mentioned above.

influenced by the teachings of the German theory: "[es] ante todo un derecho de libertad [pero también] el reconocimiento y la garantía de una institución política fundamental, que es la opinión pública libre, indisolublemente ligada con el pluralismo político, que es un valor fundamental y un requisito del funcionamiento del Estado democrático." For the creation of the media, the Court uses the classic thesis that differentiates the press from television, but refuses to intervene on the matter and entrusts the legislator with the delicate task of deciding whether to include private television in the broadcasting system. For the Spanish Court, like those of other states, the freedom to create a television medium does not derive directly from the Constitution. Moreover, it is apparent from the judgment that Article 20 does not require the state to authorize private broadcasters, but neither does it prohibit it. According to the Court, this is a "political issue" which lies with the legislator, which is free to act within the law, but constrained in the way it may act. This is perhaps the most "ambiguous" part, on which the *voto particular* of Judge Francisco Rubio Llorente insists: "decisions relating to the existence or non-existence of a freedom can never be considered political issues"; moreover, broadcasting requires the adoption of rules on the organization and "el legislador está constitucionalmente obligado a establecerlas" (Among the many: Bastida Freijedo 1987, p. 70).

The subsequent case law confirms the approach of STC 12/1982, on which all the legal framework in Spain was then built, and which again considered television to be an essential public service.

The Creation of a System: The (Compensatory) Role of the Italian Constitutional Court

Among the various anomalies of the broadcasting system, we must include the way in which Italian broadcasting initially grew: firstly, the clear absence (and not mere slowness) of the legislature, which was supposed to ensure and implement the exercise of freedom of expression, the "cornerstone of democratic order"[14] and secondly, the role of the Italian Constitutional Court which developed the broadcasting system

[14] Italian Constitutional Court, judgment 84/1969 and, in the literature, for all: Barile (1984, p. 228), Esposito (1958, p. 48), Paladin (1987, p. 14).

through a series of judgments, thus playing a para-legislative role (Pavani 2017, p. 508).

The constitutional basis for broadcasting actually appears in the first part of the Constitution, namely in Article 21 and in Articles 41 and 43, which enabled the regulation of broadcasting activities.

One of the main criticisms is that the drafting the Constitution was short-sighted, tending to a retrospective attitude when drafting Article 21 that had little in common with the international texts (e.g. Article 19 of the Universal Declaration of Human Rights of 1948) and the Constitutions of other European states in force at the time. According to some scholars, the Constituent Assembly "drew on the experiences of the past, far more than the prospects to come" (Paladin 1979, p. 6), and regulated only the active profile of the freedom of expression (and not the passive and reflective profiles) and considered the press as the only means of communication (a good analysis of the proposals in the constituent Assembly in Zaccaria 1977, p. 30*ff.*).

The interpretation of the Constitutional Court was therefore essential to build the basis of the broadcasting system; the Court filled the legal gaps with a series of judgments that were "additive, manipulative" or judgments of principle that influenced both the organizational profile as well as the activities and mission of broadcasting.

Regarding the nature and activity of broadcasting, the Court upheld the theoretical position that Article 21 of the Constitution would include the freedom to distribute, reproduce and disseminate thought all the media (judgments 59/1960 and 105/1972).[15] The Italian Constitutional Court ruled that the establishment of broadcasters descends directly from the freedom of expression (from judgment 105/1972 onwards).

[15] Regarding the nature and activity of broadcasting, the Court upheld the theoretical position that Art. 21 of the Constitution would include the freedom to distribute, reproduce and disseminate thought all the media (judgments 59/1960 and 105/1972): Crisafulli (1964, p. 297), Esposito (1958, p. 27), Paladin (1987, pp. 17, 21), and also Fois (1960, p. 1127).

The Italian Constitutional Court has ruled that the establishment of broadcasters descends directly from the freedom of expression (from judgment 105/1972 onwards).

In exercising its quasi-legislative task, the Constitutional Court was guided by a basic principle of democracy: pluralism, considered as both internal (potential openness to all the political, social and cultural forces of the country), external (so that the greatest possible number of actors and perspectives be granted access to the airwaves in order to enhance the scope of "voices" and perspectives available to the public) and substantial (respect for pluralism in the delicate moments of electoral competition): judgments 112/1993 and 466/2002.

This orientation has continued from when broadcasting was a monopoly. Indeed, in its first judgment (59/1960) the Court justified the state monopoly on the basis of a scarcity of frequencies and the danger of the formation of a private oligopoly. It did also, however, immediately express some first *warnings* to the legislature (the need to extend access to the media to the different sectors of society and the shift of guidance and control of the public broadcaster from the government to Parliament). These *indications* were to remain unheeded for more than a decade.

The 1970s were a time of savage incursions on frequencies by private enterprises: the legal vacuum on frequency planning, together with the economic recovery and technological progress, facilitated the de facto occupation of frequencies by local broadcasters (shortly after the start of private broadcasting presidential Decree 156/1973 was adopted on the "Consolidated Law regarding postal, postal banking and telecommunications services" which enshrined the exclusive right of the state to cable television systems as well. The legislation created a political crisis and led to the resignation of the Government headed by Giulio Andreotti.

The Constitutional Court confirmed the warnings that had been expressed previously in 1960, and in judgment 225/1974 laid out the so-called "Seven Commandments" that the legislator translated into Law 103/1975. This law placed the broadcasting system within the essential public service category, based on fundamental principles such as independence, objectivity and cultural openness.[16]

The intervention of the legislature came too late to regulate the existing situation as regards private broadcasters, where one business group

[16]In judgment 202/1976 the Court broke the link between the social function of television and the monopoly and admitted a mixed public-private system, based on the goal of increasing the availability of broadcasts, but open only to broadcasters at a local level, creating another anomaly compared to the situation in other European states. In fact, the Court did not perceive a risk of the formation of private monopolies or oligopolies at a local level.

had risen to dominate the others; in just a few years, its networks covered a third of the national television audience (Chapter 6).

To remedy this situation a series of decree laws were adopted, known as the "Berlusconi decrees" that later became Law 10/1985. These did no more than recognise the existing situation, while failing to implement the recommendations of the Italian Constitutional Court regarding the enforcement of the principle of pluralism ("in no way might pluralism be considered as respected at a national level, where the competition exists between a public and a private sector both represented by a single entity, and/or that enjoys a dominant position in the private sector," judgment n. 826/1988).

This prolonged period, known as the "caos dell'etere", lasted until the introduction of Law 223/1990 (the so-called "Mammì law") on the 'Regulation of the public and private broadcasting system' which provided basic rules for the broadcasting system (both public and private) and, in fact, recognized and legitimized the legislative duopoly of Fininvest-Rai.

Conclusion

Very few European Constitutions mention television among the media. Hence, the absence in some Constitutions of provisions, or even a mention, related to broadcasting, has called for an extensive interpretation of the regulations on freedom of expression. In this sense, the scholarship and Constitutional Courts have played a crucial role in guiding the legislator in the implementation of the constitutional texts. In fact, the Constitutional Courts and the Supreme Courts have played a significant role in building the "freedom of broadcasting," by contributing to the adaptation of the constitutional text to the (new) constitutional context and by establishing some of the regulatory models that have spread beyond state boundaries. At times they have played a creative (and surrogate) role. The Courts have laid down the constitutional principles to which legislators referred when creating broadcasting legislation, especially in relation to principles of pluralism and the independence of PSB. These principles have since become standards adopted by the supranational organizations (CoE and EU, see Chapter 3) and have influenced the mission and remits of public broadcasters in the different states.

References

Arenas Ramiro, M. (2015). El régimen jurídico de los medios de comunicación en Alemania. *Teoría y Realidad Constitucional, 36*, 539–588.

Arnold, R. (1997). The role of public television broadcasting within the competitive market in Germany. In S. Muñoz Machado (Ed.), *Derecho europeo del audiovisual. Actas del congreso organizado per la asocación europea de derecho del audiovisual*, Sevilla, octubre 1996, Vol. I, Madrid: Escuela libre editorial.

Barendt, E. (2005). *Freedom of speech* (2nd ed.). Oxford: Oxford University Press.

Barile, P. (1984). *Diritti dell'uomo e libertà fondamentali.* Milano: Giuffrè.

Bastida Freijedo, F. J. (1987). Las televisiones regionales en España. *Autonomies, 7*, 55–74.

Bastida Freijedo, F. J. (1998). El derecho a crear medios de comunicación social y sus límites (Prontuario de Jurisprudencia constitucional). *Aranzadi. Repertorio del Tribunal Constitucional* (Vol. IV), 351–446.

Bullinger, M. (1989). Freiheir von presse, rundfunk und film. In J. Isensee & P. Kirchhof (Eds.), *Handbuch des Staatsrechts* (Vol. VI). Heidelberg: C. F. Müller.

Crisafulli, V. (1964). Problematica della libertà di informazione. *Il Politico.*

Engelke, H. J. (1992). *Die interpretation der Rundfunkfreiheit des Grundgesetzes.* Frankfurt, Bern: Springer.

Esposito, C. (1958). *La libertà di manifestazione del pensiero nell'ordinamento italiano.* Milano: Giuffrè.

Fois, S. (1960). La libertà di diffusione del pensiero e monopolio televisivo. *Giurisprudenza costituzionale.*

González Encinar, J. J. (1996). *La televisión pública en la Unión Europea.* Madrid: Mc Graw-Hill.

González Encinar, J. J. (2000). Modelos comparados de regulación de lo audiovisual. In T. de la Quadra-Salcedo (Ed.), *El régimen jurídico del audiovisual.* Barcelona: Marcial Pons.

Hoffmann-Riem, W. (1994). Stadien des Rundfunk-Richterrechts. In O. Jarren (Ed.), *Medienwandel-Gesellschaftswandel. 10 Jahre dualer Rundfunk in Deutschland.* Berlin: Vistas.

Hoffmann-Riem, W., & Schulz, W. (1996). La televisión pública en Alemania. In J. J. González Encinar (Ed.), *La Televisión pública en la Unión Europea.* Madrid: Mc Graw-Hill.

Klotz, F. (2000). The Radio and Television System in Germany. *Radio and television systems in Europe, 2000/2001*, 123–137.

Paladin, L. (1979). Problemi e vicende della libertà di informazione nell'ordinamento giuridico italiano. In L. Paladin (Ed.), *Libertà di informazione.* Torino, UTET.

Paladin, L. (1987). Libertà di pensiero e libertà di informazione: le problematiche attuali. *Quaderni costituzionali, 1*, 5–27.

Pavani, G. (2012). *Radiotelevisioni. Profili storici e comparati*. Bologna: Filodiritto.

Pavani, G. (2017, August). Anomalies of the Italian public service broadcasting despite the law 220 of 2015. *European Public Law, 23*(3), 507–524.

Peces-Barba Martínez, G. (1999). *Curso de derechos fundamentales*. Madrid: Eudema.

Rieber-Mohn, T. (2004, September). Norway. Proposed amendments to Article 100 of the Norwegian Constitution (freedom of expression). *Iris Merlin*. Available at http://merlin.obs.coe.int/iris/2004/9/article32.en.html.

Salvador Martínez, M. (1998). *La libertad de la Televisión. El modelo alemán*. Barcelona: Cedecs.

Starck, C. (1973). Rundfunkfreiheit als Organisationsproblem. *Recht und Staat, 422/423*.

Stern, K. (1994). *Das Staatsrechts der Bundesrepublik Deutschland* (Vol. III). München: C. H. Beck.

Vigevani, G. E. (2017). *Fondamento costituzionale e autonomia dei media di servizio pubblico nell'età della rete*. Torino: Giappichelli.

von Mangoldt, H., Klein, F., & Starck, C. (1999). *Das Bonner Grundgesetz: Kommentar, Vol. I*: Präambel, Artikel 1 bis 19, 4th ed., München, Art. 5 I, II para. 100.

Zaccaria, R. (1977). *Radiotelevisione e Costituzione*. Milano: Giuffrè.

Zimmermann, R. (2011). Die Meinungsfreiheit in der neueren Rechtsprechung des Bundesverfassungsgerichts. *Neue Justiz Cuaderno, 4*.

CHAPTER 5

The Organization of the Public Broadcasters

Abstract This chapter describes the legal framework of all the EU countries with an analytical-comparative approach and focusses on two important issues to evaluate the independence and pluralism of the public broadcasters (decentralized organization of the broadcaster and method of funding). The existing wide range of solutions offers interesting insights for comparison that, starting from the data on the internal organization of the public broadcasters of the EU member states (composition of the management bodies, appointment procedure, term of office, etc.), leads to considerations on the way they operate and their relationship with state and local political institutions, namely, their governance. The cross-sectional and comparative analysis of legislation on the organization of Public service broadcasters offers a complete picture of the various solutions adopted by states.

Keywords Public service broadcasters · Decentralization · Comparative approach · Independence · Pluralism · Management bodies

Introduction

The respect of the pan-European standards discussed in Chapter 3, is leading to harmonization of PSB from a material point of view, and a sharing of principles that is gradually strengthening the public mission. On the other hand, the structure of the public broadcasters is

G. Pavani, *The Structure and Governance of Public Service Broadcasting*, https://doi.org/10.1007/978-3-319-96731-8_5

noticeably heterogeneous, as each state organizes its PSB according to its own historical, legal, economic and social traditions. Thus, a broad range of organizational solutions has appeared, often with unique features, as in the case of the Netherlands, or related to the territorial form of a decentralized state (e.g. Germany, Belgium and, in part, Spain). The link between radio and TV and the social, political, cultural and legal system of each country means that each public broadcaster reflects the language of the legal system to which it belongs and through which, in structural terms, it is formed. This situation was succinctly expressed by Debbasch at the end of the 1960s: "Les citoyens ont le droit de la Radio broadcasting qu'ils méritent" and he urged the lawyers to build a "droit de la Radio et de la television" (Debbasch 1969, p. 5).

A Wide Range of Structural Solutions

It is undeniable that certain decisions concerning the organization of public service broadcasting were influenced by certain "cultural models" expressed by the people who historically shaped TV or by the politicians who dominated the scene at the time of its birth,[1] while other experiences acted as "negative" models.[2] However, each state has regulated the structure of their broadcasting systems differently. In effect, PSB is the product of the specific circumstances of each Country and is "the outcome of a negotiation between different socio-cultural and political actors" (McDonnell 1987, p. 13) that initially led lawmakers to focus on a subjectivist (or nominalistic) conception of PSB. In many

[1] Thus, it seems clear that the presence in Hamburg (under British occupation) of Hugh Greene, future Director General of the BBC, as head of Nordwestdeutscher Rundfunk, influenced the strategic choices of German public television (Carleton Greene 1969, p. 144). The preference for the Reithian model demonstrated by Arturo Carlo Jemolo throughout his presidency of the Committee on Culture, explain the centralized structure of the Italian broadcasting system, despite the regional organization introduced with the new Constitution. Similarly, the choice in favour of monopoly in France was promptly confirmed (and strengthened) by the centralizing policies of de Gaulle in the early decades of the Fifth Republic. On historical events: Smith (1995).

[2] In the parliamentary proceedings on the proposed amendments of the Dutch system, a centralized organizational model was found to be inadvisable because of the risk of political interference so strong that it could lead to the "Berlusconian model" (*Political debates about the future of public broadcasting*, in *Hilversummary*, December 2004, 1–3).

cases, the status prevailed (the who over the what); thus, PSB equates with services carried out by public institutions, initially in a state monopoly and then operating in mixed markets (in which even private operators must respect certain obligations). There are, however, cases of broadcasting services considered in an objective (or functional) sense, whose public mission is entrusted to private companies.

A comparative analysis provides some key indications: firstly, the dominant form sees the allocation of PSB to a single company for the entire national territory. Examples of such a choice can be seen with the Finnish YLE-Oy Ylesradio, the Irish RTE-Raidió Teilifís Éireann and the Portuguese RPT-Rádio e Televisão de Portugal (*sociedade anónima*) as well as Iceland's RUV-Ríkisútvarpi and more recently the renewed Greek PSB ERT-Elliniki Radiofonía Tileórasi, that was closed for two years and temporarily replaced by the NERIT broadcaster (Nea Elliniki Radiofonía, Internet kai Tileórasi).[3]

There are fewer cases of PSB organizations being split among several companies. The reasons behind such a choice may be explained by several factors. In some countries, the territorial organization (whether decentralized or especially Federal) involves a natural division of PSB, as in Belgium or Germany where broadcasters are organized at the regional level and coordinated centrally by the relevant body. In other cases, the splitting of PSB among broadcasters is the result of political choices that have affected the corporate form (France, for a long time). Sometimes, the historical and cultural characteristics that affected the legal system led to the fragmentation of the respective radio and television systems among a number of companies. Such is the case of Sweden, where three separate companies owned by an independent public foundation pursue the mission of PSB (SVT-Sveriges Television; SR-Sveriges Radio, UR-Sveriges Utbildningsradio) and Denmark (DR-Danmarks Radio, one of the world's oldest radio and television services, founded in 1925, remained

[3]After a Government decision on 11 June 2013 to close the public broadcaster ERT, described by the Minister responsible for the Media as "a typical example of lack of transparency and incredible waste" (Statement by the Deputy Minister of the Prime Minister and Government Spokesperson, *Simos Kedikoglou*, 11 June 2013, see *Alexandros Economou*, Greek Public Broadcaster in Crisis, MMR-Aktuel l 2013, 347680—beck-online) and following a series of court appeals to contain the effects of this decision (in particular those related to employees), on 19 July 2013, the new Law N. 4173 on Radio, Television and the Internet was passed. The Law created the broadcaster NERIT that operated from May 2014 to June 2015.

a monopoly until 1988 and TV2).[4] Moreover, of special interest is the case of the Netherlands in which two companies, the older Nederlandse Omroep Stichting—NOS—founded in 1919, and the more recent NTR (born from the merger of NPS, Teleac and RVU and offering cultural, educational, ethnic, and children's programmes), have given rise to one of the most competitive and unusual television systems in Europe. Even though the Dutch market is of limited dimensions, from the outset broadcasting was considered as a vehicle that would directly ensure the consolidation of social, cultural and ideological pluralism in the country. The profound religious and cultural cleavages of the end of the nineteenth century that divided Dutch society into distinct streams (Catholic, Protestant, liberal and socialist) spilt over into the radio (and later) the television system, leading to the so-called "pillarisation"—*verzuiling*—system that functions by means of continuous "politics of accommodation" applied to all public sectors. The "umbrella" structure of the Dutch public broadcasting system was original and reflected the democratic history of this country: the public foundation NOS (Nederlandse Publieke Omroep) acts as the governing body for a number of member-based broadcasting associations, none of which has its own facilities.[5]

[4] The Social Democratic Party (Dansk Folkparti), which dominated the political scene from the post-war period to the 1980s, used the PSB as a vehicle to spread its ideals of equality of social conditions and the creation of efficient public services. When foreign satellite TV broke into the national market in 1988, Denmark responded to the break-up of its monopoly by strengthening the public sector, creating more than a second channel, but what was a actually a further public body (TV2), partly funded through advertising (decidedly ahead of the other Nordic countries). The privatization procedure that started in 2003 was sanctioned by the European Commission due to state funding of the TV2 broadcaster.

[5] In April 2012, the Dutch government adopted an amendment to Art. 2139 of the Media Act of 2008 (that came into force on 1 January 2013) that abolished the monopoly held by the public broadcasters on television programming. A key role was played by the *Commissariaat voor de Media* (Dutch Media Authority) acting on the initiative of the Ministry of Education, Culture and Science. The monopoly on programming was a legacy of the traditional Dutch pillar system, whereby broadcasters linked to political parties, churches and social movements were responsible for their own programming. Now they must communicate it to the NPO. On 14 February 2013, the Minister of Education, Culture and Science proposed a further reform of the 2008 law to modernize the public broadcasting system. Since 2016, budget cuts have led to a downsizing of NOS to 8

When the countries of Eastern Europe came to restructure their broadcasting systems they preferred to separate radio broadcasting from that of television, regulating the two with separate laws (Latvia, Czech Republic, Slovak Republic, Romania, Hungary[6]) and organizing each service (radio and television) in one public body (with rare exceptions, such as Poland, where both Telewizja Polska and Polskie Radio incorporate several public broadcasters, each organized in independent companies).[7]

operating broadcasters instead of the former 21. In addition to NOS and NTR there are to be three new cooperative broadcasters and three new independent broadcasters. The "depillarisation" of Dutch society is also the result of cultural factors: in the same period, the entry into the market of new broadcasting associations that aim primarily to provide entertainment (symbolized by Radio Veronica) has dismantled the foundations of the broadcasting system.

[6]This is the way it was until 1 January 2015, the date of entry into force of the amendment to the Hungarian Media Act by which a new subject, Médiaszolgáltató Részvénytársaság Dune (Dune Media Service), replaced Televízió Magyar (Hungarian Television), Duna Televízió (Duna TV), Magyar Rádió (Hungarian radio) and Magyar Távirati Iroda (Hungarian News Agency), and became the provider for all the television, public radio and online content services. In fact, the merger into a single provider did not change the previous structure of the media, because the main actor of the Hungarian public broadcasters remained the Médiaszolgáltatás-támogató és Vagyonkezelő Alap (MTVA, Media Services and Support Trust Fund).

[7]Examples of broadcasters having a public legal nature are: Eesti Rahvusringhääling (ERR) in Estonia; Latvian Radio and Latvian Television (defined in Art. 57, para. 2 of the first law on the broadcasting system in 1995 "State non-profit companies with limited liability"); Lietuvos ir nacionalinio radijo Televizijos (LRT) in Lithuania ("non-profit public broadcaster," according to Law n. I-1571, 1996); Czech Television in the Czech Republic (for Art. 1, Law 83/1991 'is a legal person managing its own property whose principal part is the property transferred from Czechoslovak Television'; Art. 1 of the 2005 Regulations provides that "Czech Television is a legal entity established as of 1 January 1992 by Act No. 483/1991 Coll., on Czech Television. Czech Television is a public institution operating television broadcasting"); Slovak Television in the Slovak Republic (Art. 2, para. 1 of the 2004 law states that it "is a public, national, independent institution providing public television broadcasting services in the fields of information, culture and education. (2) Slovak Television is a legal entity registered in the commercial register"); the Slovenian RTV Slovenia (Art. 2, para. 1 law of 2005 "is an independent legal person of special cultural and national importance governed by public law" and para. 4 "the only founder and owner of RTV Slovenia is the Republic of Slovenia") and Hungary (even after the 2015 amendments).

"Regional" Television

All the European experiences show some form of decentralization, in the widest sense, of broadcasting.[8] Such decentralization permits the protection of regional identities (including cultural, linguistic and religious identities), facilitates the spread of information throughout the state territory while strengthening democratic participation at every level of government. "Media operating at the regional level have special democratic significance as the relationship between regional media and persons from the areas and communities they serve tends to be closer than equivalent relationships at, for example, the national or international levels" (European Audiovisual Observatory 2016, p. 11).

In a technological landscape that embodies the slogan "any content, anytime, anywhere, any platform" and where local and global combine, regional television broadcasters can redefine their borders and their production—just like national broadcasters—thus spreading knowledge and information within the local community and beyond its confines and telling the greater story through a thousand smaller stories, as Morawski expressed it (Morawski 2005, p. 9).

Regional television networks are therefore supported by European organizations and various bodies of the Council of Europe have adopted standards, some legally binding and some politically influential, to create such an enabling environment for regional media.[9]

[8] It is necessary to specify that I here use the term "regional" for generic references to TV stations operating in a subnational level of government, intermediate between the state and local authorities (*Regioni*, *Comunidades Autónomas*, *Länder*, etc.). When referring to individual countries I will contextualize PSB in the respective territorial law, remaining faithful to the terminology proper to that Country (e.g. the term "state" may refer to the TV of the member states of a federal state). I will not discuss "local" TV stations (namely those operating in a territorial area corresponding to a Municipality or Province, where such exists) because these are generally private televisions and radio stations.

[9] The general principles concerning pluralism, participation, the media democracy of Art. 10 ECHR are also relevant for regional audiovisual media, as the European Court of Human Rights has stressed (*Gorzelik and Others v. Poland* [GC], no. 44158/98, §92, ECHR 2004-I). Documents devoted to the protection of minorities such as the Framework Convention for the Protection of National Minorities (FCNM) and the European Charter on Regional or Minority Language (ECRML) consider the regional media as forms of promotion and protection of minorities.

At a European level, the Treaties do not provide the EU with explicit competence for freedom of expression or for the pluralism of the regional media. However, the same considerations noted earlier on EU policies that facilitate state broadcasters can be extended to regional media, (Chapter 3). Such interest is further confirmed by a recent project co-financed by the EU, aimed at monitoring media pluralism at both national and regional levels. Early results of this comparative analysis on PSM that regularly broadcast regional programmes in 19 EU countries notes that "none of the countries fulfilled all of the four safeguards considered, and that six of the countries were at a high risk by fulfilling only one of four safeguard mechanisms."[10]

Despite the support of the European organizations, negative trends are apparent in the panorama of regional PSB (which go beyond the results of the project just mentioned), such as the closure of *Radio Televisión Valenciana* (RTVV) in 2013 (*Corporació Valenciana de Mitjans de Comunicació* was to take over in 2016); the closure of four regional programmes of Bălgarska Nacionalna Televizija—Bulgarian National Television—due to the introduction of digitalisation and "the lack of any private investor's interest to develop a regional multiplex broadcasting these programmes" (Nikolova 2016) as well as the structural reform of regional audiovisual media in the Netherlands in order to reduce the public funding of regional broadcasters by 1 January 2017, transferring the funding of regional broadcasting from the provincial authorities to central government.[11] This trend has been confirmed among private TV broadcasters (in Sweden, the commercial broadcaster TV4 closed all 25 local and regional stations in 2014).

[10]The Media Pluralism Monitor (MPM) project is carried out by the Centre for Media Pluralism and Media Freedom (CMPF) at the European University Institute. As regards the role of PSM, the four standards considered are: the involvment of the local community in the production and distribution of content; national news available in local languages; local correspondents; a balance of journalists from different geographical areas (http://cmpf.eui.eu/media-pluralism-monitor/).

[11]The reform began with the amendment of the Media Act 2008 proposed by the Ministry of Education, Culture and Science (Regulation of the State Secretary for Education, Culture and Science, 11 June 2014, n. WJZ/634652 (10487).

Territorial Forms of State and the Decentralized Organization of PSB

The broadcasting system is naturally an offshoot of each Country's history; regional TV are more subject to the internal dynamics and the centrifugal or centripetal thrusts that characterize the territorial form of the state (centralized or decentralized) than the national ones.

The "mosaic" (Garitaonandía 2000, p. 41), of regional TV broadcasters, is rather complex and lends itself to both a "vertical" and "horizontal" comparison (Konijnenbelt 1994, p. 121*ff.*). A vertical comparison can be conducted in countries with strong territorial decentralization where there are several regional public broadcasters, either associated at the national level (e.g. Germany) or operating separately (e.g. Belgium) or that share the territory with decentralized branches of the national PSB (e.g. Spain). Such an analysis is helpful to understand the similarities and differences between the public broadcasters of the different local entities and allows comparison with the national PSB. Moreover, it allows identification of the objects to be compared—thus satisfying the requirement of comparability—and justifies a comparison between apparently non-homogeneous objects: (formally) regional public broadcasters with the state public broadcasters of unitary states.

It should be noted, however, that the (horizontal) comparison of the organization of public broadcasters reflects the tendencies of political decentralization apparent in most modern democratic states, summarized in the statement "every state is decentralized in its own way" (Vandelli 2017, p. 23). In fact, it is unlikely today to group the processes of decentralization into rigid and monothetic classes because the variables exceed the invariables identified over time by the scholarship, and the experience of each state exhibits some element of diversity. Such differences may be present in the separation of the legislative competences between the central and local entities, the formation of the second Chamber and participation in the exercise of state powers, etc. This variety of solutions makes any basis for the analysis of the law rather shaky and calls into question classifications based solely on normative parameters linked to the territorial form of the state.[12]

[12] I will therefore use the categories of federal, regional and unitary states in a descriptive and non-prescriptive perspective.

The legal analysis (of domestic law), generally follows a top-down parabola: mostly it is limited to identifying the provider of the television service (public or private), studying the division of legislative competences between the centre and the periphery, analysing regulation of the television service by the two levels of government and highlighting the organizational aspects. A clear example is provided by the somewhat dated study by Rosado Iglesias on the systems of Germany, Austria, Belgium, Canada, Spain and the UK. Despite the Author's effort to frame the competences in two overriding types (participation in the management of broadcasting services, on the one hand, and direct provision of services through regional channels, on the other), it responds to the top-down parabola (Rosado Iglesias 1998, p. 237*ff.*).

This approach is appropriate to the historically federal states in which the establishment of the public broadcasters and the federative process have developed in parallel, and where both are the result of a bottom-up process (as in Germany, where the *Länder* are responsible for enacting broadcasting legislation ex-arts. 30 and 70.1 of the Constitution, and their public broadcasters are joint in a consortium and share programming across the network and on the national channel ARD), or in states whose federative structure is characterized by strong linguistic identities and the PSB contribute to the implementation of cultural functions that belong to the respective Communities (as in Belgium where the three communities—Flemish, French and German-speaking—each have normative competence for audiovisual communication and have their own PSB, namely VRT, RTBF.Be and BRF, respectively).

However, the broadcasting system does not always reflect the decentralized organization of all federal states. In Austria, for example, ORF is the national PSB and has regional studios in the nine Federal Provinces that produce their own radio programmes as well as regional TV news which are broadcast in the local window of ORF 2. On the other hand, the broadcasting system may reflect a single element as in Switzerland, where SRG-SSR (the national PSB) includes four sub-units corresponding to the four languages spoken in the Cantons.

In regional states, the solutions may differ greatly. In Spain (only formally a non-federal state), most of the *Comunidades Autónomas* have their own television stations and are responsible for the implementation of freedom of expression in their territories (the 2012 reform allows regional public service broadcasters greater flexibility in the provision of their audiovisual media services: the *Comunidades Autónomas* may opt for a direct or indirect management of their PSBs through various models, including public-private partnership). The channels of the twelve, autonomous regional public broadcasters together formed a federation (*Federación de Organismos o Entidades de Radio y Televisión Autonómicos*). The organization in distinct regional public broadcasting companies is similar to that of Federal states as Belgium, but the same degree of decentralization cannot be found in the national PSB which is organized in 17 regional windows of the RTVE.

In Italy, a state with strong regionalism on paper (namely in its Constitution), the legislative competence of the Regions in the field of communications is totally obscured by the national legislator, thanks also to the support of the Constitutional Court. In fact, RAI's regional offices are not regional TV stations but rather regional public service channels of the national PSB.

By contrast, in the UK—a historically unitary state that has recently seen a devolution of power—television decentralization is a culturally rooted concept (ITV, the Network with public obligations was born in a decentralized form). Moreover, the BBC has a decentralized structure in the Nations.

However, there is no homogeneity even among unitary states (where the local authorities do not have legislative powers); indeed, there is a broad range of circumstances. There are cases of weak decentralization of the organization of the national PSB when it operates at a regional level through regional public channels (RTV in Slovenia, TVP3 in Poland, ERT3 in Greece, TVT3 in Romania) or regional "windows," some broadcast in time slots of the national PSB (BNT2 in Bulgaria, CT in Czech Republic, TV 2 in Denmark). Alternatively, there are cases in which the regional studios of public broadcasters do not fill a broadcast time slot of PSB, however, they produce programming used on national services and contribute to news reports on national TV (RTÉ in Ireland, MTVA in Hungary that operates with 2 regional studios that produce the majority of ethnic minority programming). There are also cases in which no regional PSB is identified as in Estonia, Iceland, Latvia, Lithuania, Luxemburg and Malta. Finally, the case of the Netherlands stands as an exception, with 13 separate regional public broadcasters that operated via the ROOS foundation until the law reform of March 2016 in which the government transferred the administrative and financial responsibility of the regional broadcasters to the central government and reduced their budget.

The decentralization of PSB cannot, therefore, be measured only in terms of normative competences corresponding to the territorial entities of the state. The most striking example is the organizational "model" of distinct regional public broadcasting companies, which would seem fitting only for federal states, or those with strong regionalism (like Belgium and Spain), and is instead adopted in the Netherlands as well.

To appreciate the actual degree of "proximity" of a public broadcaster to a territorial collectivity, other factors must be assessed such as the contribution of the regional output to national television and the degree of independence of the regional media compared to the national ones. In order to deduce the level of independence, we must consider the breadth of their activity, their relationships with the territorial institutions and their funding constraints, and so on. Unless we are familiar with the programming of regional TV networks it will be difficult to understand the regulatory provisions related to the protection of minorities, respect for the native language and the promotion of local culture, which appear in all laws on broadcasting systems of decentralized countries (and not only these).

It is, therefore, necessary to master concepts that move beyond legal canons and to draw on data derived from studies in other sciences such as sociology and the science of communication and to use them as tools for a legal framework. While such studies take into account the classifications on decentralization frameworks (that provide macro-areas of reference), their methodologies are based on a bottom-up process that starts from individual television experiences to then derive common elements. The level of interaction between the sciences will, of course, depend on the sensitivity of the comparatist, but we must recognize the need to do more than simply refer to extra-legal data, although this is useful for a better understanding of the context in which the research is conducted (e.g. to understand the Dutch system of pillarization). By integrating the results of studies using parameters such as television "production" (Garitaonandía 2000),[13] or a combination of legal and

[13]This made it possible to outline the following regional television models (of both public and private broadcasters): (1) "Deconcentrated television" (production output by regional TV stations dependent on central management decisions, e.g. ERT in Greece prior to its closure); (2) "Decentralized television" (regional television stations produce local news programmes and collaborate on the production of reports for central news programmes, e.g. RAI 3 in Italy, RTVE in Spain); (3) "Regional television" (production

extra-legal parameters (Richeri 2005, p. 46*ff.*),[14] it is possible to include those states that from a legal perspective of division of legislative competences in the field of broadcasting and communication, can be classified as unitary (states that have opted for regional public service channels or regional windows of the national PSB such as Poland, Greece and Romania) in the class of decentralized PSB.

output by regional TV stations is greater than model 2 and includes cultural, entertainment and sports programmes, e.g. BBC Scotland or TVE Catalunya); (4) "Federal television" (regional stations that produce programmes for the national broadcasting system and extended programmes for their own regions, working or broadcasting as members of the national channel or central network, e.g. the German *Länder*); (5) "Autonomous television" (independent regional television stations that broadcast their own programmes across their respective regions, e.g. the Spanish autonomous channels); (6) "Supra-regional, national and/or international regional television" (regional TV stations that broadcast not only for their own region but also at a more extended level, be it national or international, via satellite, to other parts of Europe, e.g. the third channel of certain German *Länder* broadcast via the Astra satellite to other *Länder* and in Europe, as well as some Spanish autonomous channels broadcast via the Hispasat satellite or the channels RTBF e BRT of the Belgian communities); and (7) "Local regional TV" (regional television stations operating at a more "localized" level and generally private). This classification is still broadly viable, while certain parts have acquired historical value (due to the transition to digital terrestrial television). For further detail: Garitaonandía and Moragas (1995), based on the leading research of scholars of Communication studies such as: Stephane (1983), Musso (1991), Zimmerman (1990), and Garitaonandía (1993, pp. 277–294).

[14] In the research on regional public broadcasters (commissioned by Circom Regional at the Media and Journalism Institute of the Faculty of Communication Sciences of the University of Italian Switzerland), for each state the following were analysed: the regulatory framework; the territorial level of television coverage; the structure of the organization(s); the means of financing; audience results; the prospects of digitization. The results were processed on the basis of some parameters such as: (a) the independence of the regional broadcasters from the national television stations (as in Spain, Germany, Denmark, the Netherlands and Portugal) as opposed to decentralization (this is the case, among others, of Italy, the United Kingdom and France), to point out that there are "composite situations that vary from case to case"; (b) programming, namely "the degree to which regional offices are used for national activities" (this category includes experiences of federal states such as Switzerland, and "regional" states such as Spain and the United Kingdom, and tendentially centralized states like France and Sweden); (c) relations with regional institutions (the reference is to the interference and the degree of control exercised by the level of government corresponding to the television company (e.g. the power of appointment exercised by regional assemblies, as well as participation in the financing of public broadcasters); and (d) the breadth of regional activity (again, under other guises, the difference is present between television organizations that manage their own television channels and the regional offices of broadcasters).

In the same way, it is possible to exclude from the class of decentralized public broadcasters (at least the class with a highly decentralized organization) some federal and regional states with a strong decentralization on paper, whose local entities have (or rather, should have) legislative powers regarding broadcasting and communications (e.g. Italy).

To do this, you need a certain flexibility in creating the classes given that a single country can simultaneously be assigned to several groups. For example, in Spain there are 17 regional windows of the national public broadcaster RTVE (a solution generally adopted in the unitary states or countries with weak political decentralization) and there are 12 autonomous regional public broadcasters (governed by the *Comunidades Autónomas*), whereas regional channels such as RAI3 in Italy and France 3 in France serve both as regional public service channels and regional windows of the national public broadcasters.

The Internal Structure of Public Broadcasters

The fragmentation of the structural setup of PSB makes any attempt to classify the different experience of separate states difficult, but at the same time offers interesting insights for comparison that go beyond the mere organizational aspects of the bodies managing the PSB or their composition, by also taking into account the way they operate, their relationship with state and local political institutions, or more simply, their governance.

A first comparative analysis, based on the "legal formant," can identify some common trends regarding the internal organization of the public broadcasters.

Broadly speaking, the most simplified form of their management structure looks like this:

- a collegial body (hereinafter, generically referred to as the "Board," apart from the cases where the specific linguistic terms reflect a different composition and role of the body);
- a monocratic body, responsible for operational management (hereinafter Director-General or President, with the above caveats); not infrequently there are collegial executive bodies that flank or replace the monocratic organ.

Sometimes there is an additional body present alongside these in the form of a group representing the "partners" and/or "users" that has no executive responsibilities but in some way forms part of the Board.

Usually, the Director-General/President is elected by the Board and maintains a fiduciary relationship with it. In these cases, the method of appointment and the characteristics of the Board influence the executive body by affecting its autonomy and its level of independence from the political class.

According to national regulations, such bodies are assigned certain roles and various functions that can be summarized as follows:

- The Board is the body responsible for: fulfilling the overall objectives and respecting the principles related to the programming and administration assigned to it; the Board appoints and, generally, revokes the executive body (and, where present, the Directors of the regional/ local departments, where local authorities or bodies do not intervene directly) and the bodies of any companies/legal entities affiliated with the main body as well as supervising their work, in addition to the appointment of the members of any specific bodies/advisory Committees of which it makes use during the period of its mandate and whose remuneration it will decide; the setting of the institution's main principles, especially on topics related to programming, production, the insertion of advertising and funding programmes, staffing decisions, and so on; it approves the internal provisions and general rules on its own operation and that of affiliated companies/parties, as well as publishing agreements; it monitors compliance with the public service mission, whose objectives, mandates and constraints are contained in a document—usually signed with the competent Ministry—which specifies the legislation on broadcasting; it approves an annual/biannual report on the public broadcaster's work.
- The Director-General and/or President is responsible for editorial, operational and managerial functions conducted according to the general objectives and under the supervision of the Board; he/she is the legal representative of the body and stipulates contracts and agreements on issues coming under his/her authority; without interfering in Board areas, he/she implements the acts of the Board, participates in the preparation of financial reports, share capital changes, the management of the body, its offices and any

subsidiary companies; he/she proposes the institution's basic organization for Board approval, including the appointment of directors (unless he/she nominates these independently) and, in general, performs a number of routine activities.

These bodies in charge of the management, editorial responsibility and the strategic choices of PSB are flanked by others with a mainly advisory role; bodies representing—in the broadest sense—the users of radio and television; bodies for the control of editorial policy and reporting (these may frequently be from the body of journalists), etc. (e.g. the *Conselho de opinião* in Portugal, composed of "members indicated by the associations and other bodies representative of the different sectors of public opinion" ex Article 5, L. 8/2007; the *Consejo Asesor* "participating body in the company of Corporación RTVE," ex-Article 23 of Law 17/2006, composed of 15 members representing different organizations—themselves expressions of civil society—such as the *Consejo de Consumidores y Usuarios*, the *Consejo de la Juventud de España*, the *Instituto de la Mujer*, and Spanish *Consejos de Informativos*, "internal participating bodies of media professionals of the Corporación RTVE to oversee the independence, objectivity and veracity of the news content broadcast by the public service broadcaster," ex Article 24; the *Conseil consultatif des programs*, created within France Télévisions ex-Article 46, as amended by Article 22 of *Loi* n. 2009-258, composed of television viewers and charged with issuing opinions and recommendations on the programmes; the four British Audience Councils, set up by the new Royal Charter, consulted on the promotion of public targets by the BBC).

As mentioned above, the Parliament may have slightly greater weight in the appointment of the institution's Board with respect to the government and other institutional bodies, or organizations related to civil society. This is the case in Denmark where 6 of the 11 members of the DR Board are appointed by the Folketing in proportion to the political parties represented there, while in Finland all 21 members of the YLE Board are selected by the Parliament during the first session, hold office for the duration of its term (four years) and can be re-elected. In Italy (after the Law 220/2015) 4 out of 7 members of the RAI Board will be elected by the Parliament (2 by the Senate and 2 by the Chamber of Deputies), in Spain all 10 members of the RTVE Boards are elected by the Parliament (after the Law 5/2017): 4 by the Senate and 6 by Congress; in Switzerland 2 of the 9 members of the Board are appointed by the Federal Council.

In some cases, a number of parliamentarians themselves were appointed to the Board: in France (before the reform), 2 of the 14 members were appointed respectively by the parliamentary Committee on Cultural Affairs of the National Assembly and the Senate (Article 47, para. 1 *Loi* 2009-258). After the Reform of 2013, only 2 members of the Board are appointed by the Cultural Commission of National Assembly and the Senate.

The Parliament takes part, however, only indirectly in the forming of the Austrian Board: 6 members are appointed by the Federal Government in proportion to the number of seats the political parties hold in the National Assembly. In Ireland, the Parliament proposes to the competent Minister the names of 4 of the 12 members (the list is presented by the Oireachtas Joint Committee on Communications, Energy and Natural Resources). In Sweden also, the Parliament submits to the government a list of names proposed by the parties (not only on the basis of political affiliation but also on their experience in the field) and the government appoints the 13 members (including the President) of the Board of the *Förvaltningsstiftelsen för Sveriges Radio*.

The government's presence is still significant in some countries: in Austria governmental appointment applies to 9 members of the total 35 (in addition to the 6 members appointed in proportion to the composition of the National Assembly as specified above); in Denmark, 3 out of 11 of DR, including the President, are appointed by the Ministry of Culture; in France, 5 out of 14 are "*représentants de l'Etat*"; in Ireland, 6 out of 12 are nominated by the Minister of Communication; 2 of 7 in Italy will be appointed by the Minister of Economy and Finance; in Portugal, 2 of 6 members of the Board are elected by the government; in Norway 6 out of 9, including the Director-General and Deputy Director-General, are selected by the government (by the General Assembly, given that the NRK's capital is 100% state-owned), in Greece, the Board of the new ERT is appointed by the Minister of state following a public appointments process and an opinion issued by the parliamentary Committee on Institutions and Transparency.

The case of the UK has always had unique connotations. The 2007 Royal Charter established that "The Queen, on advice from government ministers and an independent commissioner for public appointments, appoints its 12 trustees." The composition of the Trust was almost identical to that of the Board of Governors. The new structure envisages a single organ, the Board (Article 19 (1)) Royal Charter 2016 of 14 members, that must consist of a number of non-executive members (including the Chair) and a number of executive members. The total number of members must be 14 (Article 21 (1)). In addition to the Chair, the non-executive members are the four Nation Members and five other members. The executive members of the Board must be the Director-General and three other members (Article 21 (3)). Only the Chair and the four Nation Members are appointed by Order in Council through a public process that should guarantee the principle of transparency. The remaining Board members, both executive and non-executive are chosen by a Nominations Committee of the Board itself (Article 31). Thus, appointment by government that was envisaged for both the Governors and the Trust no longer exists.

In addition to Parliament and government, other institutions participate in forming the Board; this occurs in federal states through the intervention of local authorities, regardless of the degree of decentralization adopted in the Country.

The weakness of Austrian federalism is reflected in the composition of the Board of ORF, the national public broadcaster that is organized in a centralized manner: the *Länder*, in fact, choose 9 members out of 35.

Where federalism functions more intensely the consequences are evident.

In Germany, the Boards of public broadcasters are composed differently from *Land* to *Land*, consisting of members from the so-called "Relevant social groups" (unions, churches, cultural and sports associations, universities, etc.). They are called upon to represent not sectorial interests but the whole civil society and identified by the legislative bodies of the *Länder*, in accordance with the principle of independence of the supervisory bodies from the executive. Obviously, it is difficult to ensure the representation of all social groups in the territory. The legislator of the *Land* enjoys a degree of discretion on the admission of groups (BVerfGE 83, 238, 334 (1991)). They elect the Director-General (*Intendent*) independently. As for the two national channels, only ZDF provides for an administrative body that is not derived directly from the regional broadcasters (the Board elects the Director-General and is composed of 60 members from different backgrounds: representatives of 16 *Länder*, political parties, the main religious denominations). The 17th Inter-State Broadcasting Agreement amending the ZDF Inter-State Agreement, adopted in 2015, contains new rules on the guarantee of independence from government, including provisions on avoiding conflicts of interest for governing body members (para. 1) and a list of people who are not permitted to join the Television Council (para. 3). These particularly include members of the European Parliament, European Commission, German Parliament, Federal Government and *Land* Governments. The number of members has been reduced from 77 to 60, and the number of Federal Government representatives from 3 to 2.

In Belgium, the Boards of the Flemish, French and German Communities public broadcasters are appointed by the corresponding Community Council (RTBF.Be and VRT) and Executives (BRF), chosen in compliance with the law on the Cultural pact and thus respecting the proportional representation of the recognized political groups in Parliament. In Switzerland also, the legal nature of SRG-SSR is a result of the Country's federal structure; it is actually an association that gathers together four distinct companies, each representative of the linguistic regions. The bodies are an expression of the regional delegations. The Assembly of Delegates comprises 41 members: 36 representatives from the 4 "regional" companies (including the 4 regional Presidents who are compulsorily delegates and members of the Executive Board) and another 5 members (3 Board members elected by the Assembly of delegates and 2 Board members chosen by the Federal Board); the Executive Board has nine members: four Presidents of the regional companies, who are *ex officio* members; 3 members appointed by the Assembly of Delegates, including the President of the Board; 2 other board members appointed by the Federal Council. Both bodies thus reflect the presence of the representative branch of the Cantonal Parliament (the Federal Council) and, above all, of the four regional companies that comprise and create the TV broadcaster itself.

Even some non-federal (or regional) countries have decentralized forms for their broadcasting systems. This feature can be noted, for example, in the composition of the Boards of the various regional TV stations that form the Danish "regional" TV2, as well as in the governing body of the broadcaster.

In addition to local institutions, a fairly common form of appointment of members of the Board is the participation of employees from the broadcaster itself, in ways that ensure the transparency and representativeness of the appointment process. In Denmark, 2 members out of the 11 on the DR Board and 2 out of 7 for that of TV2 are elected from the employees; in Finland, 2 additional members (out of a total of 21) of YLE may attend and speak at Board meetings, but have no voting rights; in France, 2 out of 14 are representatives of the staff[15]; in Ireland, 1 out of 12 are from the staff of RTE while in Norway there are 3 staff members out of the 9 on the NRK Board; In Italy, after the Law 220/2015, 1 member will be nominated by an Assembly of all the company's employees who have held a contract of employment for at least three consecutive years.

Enriching the range of those involved in the formation of the management bodies are, among others, the French *Conseil supérieur de l'audiovisuel* (CSA), the *Conselho de opinão* in Portugal; two auxiliary bodies in Austria, the afore-mentioned General Assemblies in some countries (e.g. Switzerland) and the new Supervisory Board set up in Greece for the temporary NERIT.[16]

The term of office of each body usually varies between three and five years (much depends on the relationship with the legislative body where this intervenes, prevalently the Parliament), but there are examples of shorter mandates (three years in Italy; in Norway the 6 "government-appointed" members remain in office for two years, while the 3 elected by the employees only 1 year) as well as longer ones (eight years in Sweden for the collegial body and four for the Director-General; six years in Spain), as well as partial mid-term changes (e.g. in and in Portugal half of the Board is renewal every 3).

In some cases, re-election is allowed.

As regards the monocratic (and/or collegial) executive body responsible for daily management and in charge of implementing policy (CEO), certain trends are apparent. The Director-General is chosen from among those on the governing body in Austria, and can be removed with a 2/3

[15]Elected pursuant to Titre II of Loi n. 83-675 of 26 July 1983 "*relative à la démocratisation du secteur public*".

[16]One of the foremost innovations was the creation of a supervisory council to ensure the independence from the Government of the new public broadcaster, responsible for drawing up a five-year strategic plan, the adoption of a favourable opinion on the budget proposal and the final decision on the nominations of Board members. The members of the Supervisory Board are chosen as follows: the first step is the issue of a public call and the drafting of a list of candidates to be submitted to the Minister in charge, who then proposes the names of 7 members. The final decision is taken by simple majority in a parliamentary committee formed by the President and the Vice-Presidents of the Chamber, the President of the Commission itself and the leaders of the political parties. The Board and the Director-General of NERIT are selected among the candidates who responded to the call launched by the President of the Supervisory Council.

majority; in Denmark, for both DR, although it is a collegial body, and for TV2; in Norway; in Italy with the reform approved in December 2015, the Director-General is nominated by the Board at the proposal of the Assembly of shareholders; in Ireland he/she is appointed with the consent of the government, a consent necessary also to revoke the appointment; in Germany—albeit with the caveats related to the Federal state—the Director-General of the broadcasters of the *Länder* are appointed by the Boards.

In other cases, the nomination by the Board members is indirect because of the intermediation of a collegiate body with supervisory and executive functions. Such is the case in Finland, where the Board elects an Executive College (responsible for different areas of programming: news, entertainment, children's programmes, etc.) that, in turn, elects and, if appropriate, revokes, a Director-General, and in Belgium where the Chief executive officer of VRT is elected by a collegial body (the members of which, we repeat, are appointed by the Flemish Community government).

The appointment of the administrative and managerial body in the UK has always been rather complex. During the last Royal Charter, alongside the Chair of the Executive Board (appointed by the BBC Trust) there was also a collegial body (the Executive Board), whose appointment depended on the composition of the body itself (executive members and non-executive members) and, above all, on the role of the Chair. If the Chair were also the Director-General of the BBC, this person would head a Commission responsible for proposing to the Board the names of the executive members and would have a large margin of discretion. The new structure envisages that only the Chair and the four Nation Members are appointed by Order in Council through a public process that should guarantee the principle of transparency.

In other circumstances, the appointment of the President/Director-General is an expression of the constitutional bodies. Spain's Congress of Deputies directly appoints an Executive Chairperson from among the 10 members of the Board who, in turn, is also Director-General of the *Corporación* RTVE. In France, the President of *France Télévisions* (like those of *Radio France* and the *Société en charge de l'Audiovisual extérieur de la France*) was appointed by a decree of France's President, after obtaining the approval of the *Conseil supérieur de l'audiovisuel* and the Commission for Cultural Affairs of the two Chambers for a period of five years; Article 47, para. 5—declared unconstitutional by the *Conseil*

Constitutionnel with Decision n. 2009-577 DC of March—envisaged the same procedure for the withdrawal of the tenure. *Loi* 2013-1028 of 15 November 2013 relating to the independence of the public broadcaster introduced some changes: now the President is chosen by the CSA by a majority of its members. The term of office of the body varies from three to six years.

The preference for parliamentary appointment is also confirmed in Eastern European countries where it is sometimes the only appointee of the administrative body (Estonia, Czech Republic, the Slovak Republic, flanked by a Supervisory Committee for economic and financial issues; in Romania, as confirmed by the reform approved in November 2017 by the Senate, the law has been brought into line with the Constitutional Court's decision of 12 July 2017). In other cases, alongside parliamentary appointment there exists that of the independent regulatory and supervisory authorities of the sector and organizations representing civil society (Lithuania, Slovenia; in Hungary an additional member is appointed by the Media Council). By contrast, the Act of 30 December 2015 amending the Broadcasting Act (the "Interim Act") introduces fundamental changes to the Radio and Television Broadcasting Act of 20 December 1992 (hereinafter referred to as the "Broadcasting Act"), conferring upon the Minister of state Treasury the sole competence to appoint and dismiss members of the Management and Supervisory Boards. The Constitutional Court has ruled this reform to be unconstitutional because it deprives the National Broadcasting Council of any influence over the process of electing members of the bodies of state-owned broadcasting companies.

When there is a single-person executive body, this figure is almost always referred to as the Director-General and is selected from among the Board members (this is the case, e.g. in Lithuania, where the Director-General is elected with the support of at least half of the members; in the Czech and the Slovak Republics, Slovenia, etc.; in Hungary in appointed by the Media Council).

When the body is collegial, appointments are made by the Board with the participation of other institutions. For example, in Slovenia, the Executive Board consists of 5 members appointed by the Board on a proposal from the Director-General who chairs the collegial body; in turn, the Director-General is appointed by the Board on a proposal of the Supervisory Board.

The tenure of the Directors and of the managing bodies generally lasts between three and five years.

Regardless of the mode of appointment, members of the governing bodies of public service broadcasting must have a number of requirements that are precisely laid out in the respective laws, to ensure independence of conduct throughout their mandate (this is particularly true for the members of the Board and for those of the various supervisory boards)[17] as well as well-established expertise in the field of communication and management of complex organizations (for Directors-General and members of the Boards who assist them).[18]

Funding Methods

Funding of PSB is a hotly debated topic both at a national and supranational level, not only for its economic implications but also for the institutional and political implications that it entails.

The method of funding reflects the relations between the state and the society as well as those of the culture and market of a Country and is closely connected to the role played by PSB as a means of communication and influence on public opinion. The balance between public and private sources of funding is one of the criteria for assessing the independence of PSB from political power on the one hand, and the yoke of large commercial enterprises, on the other (as the Council of Europe's Commissioner for Human Rights recently confirmed on 2 May 2017, with a new Human Rights Comment on "Public service broadcasting under threat in Europe").

[17] Incompatibilities with office in constitutional bodies or membership of certain institutions directly or indirectly related to the broadcasting industry are precisely regulated (e.g. in the Czech Republic, the members of the Czech TV Board cannot concurrently be "members of Bank Council of the Czech National Bank, any public administration employee, member of the Council of the Czech Republic for Radio and Television Broadcasting, member of the Czech Radio Council, member of the Czech Press Agency Council, Director General of Czech Radio, member of the Supervisory Commission of Czech Television or Czech Radio"); shareholders/owners of any company or companies operating in the communication sector or persons with previous criminal convictions. Often, nationality requirements are specified (e.g. Bulgaria, Lithuania, Hungary).

[18] The principal constraints for the office of Director-General include membership of political parties, which must be suspended for the duration of tenure. Frequently there are also specific requirements for holding this position (degree, specialization) and a period of experience in agencies and organizations working in the field.

However, state sovereignty has been progressively eroded by the standards imposed on European states by the EU and by the CoE (Chapter 3).

The analysis of national law highlights a varied panorama regarding the tools for funding PSB, both of a public kind (licence fee and other public funds such as state budget/grants, taxes on goods and services) and of a commercial nature (advertising and other commercial incomes as sponsorship, programme sale, merchandising, Pay TV-Radio).[19]

In an attempt to summarize, we can identify two main methods of funding, depending on whether there is a licence fee (with or without advertising) or another form of public funding (with or without advertising).

1. The Scandinavian Countries rank among those that historically finance their broadcasters with a licence fee, and generally have no advertising. In Denmark, the two public broadcasters are financed differently: TV2 with advertising and other commercial resources (some regional TV2 services receive public funds); DR with the licence fee alone. In Sweden, the fee also finances the public radio service (SR) and the Swedish Educational Broadcasting company (UR).[20] Norway has confirmed the licence fee as well as the ban on advertising (a minimum amount of commercial activity is allowed[21]), while Finland abolished the fee and replaced it with a tax on individual incomes.[22] The UK, whose traditional exclusion of advertising has its roots in the history of the BBC, has retained the licence fee though this historic PSB has opened to other resources, both public and commercial. The commercial services are managed by BBC Worldwide, the BBC's for-profit arm that operates internationally).[23] From 2018, Belgium has chosen

[19] Data are taken from the EBU Funding of Public Service Media Report 2016 e EBU Licence Fee Report 2017.

[20] Revenues are broken down as follows: licence fee 96%; other commercial revenue 2%; other revenue 2%.

[21] Act relating to broadcasting and audiovisual on-demand services (the Broadcasting Act), last amended by Act 2015-06-19-65. Revenues are as follows: licence fee 97.2% commercial activities 2.3%.

[22] Law n. 472/2012 modifying the Act on the State Television and Radio Fund.

[23] From January 2017, the fee is governed by the new Agreement which includes some changes, such as the removal of the licence fee for over 75s with an estimated cost of GBP

to confirm a reduced licence fee for RTFB. Be and the revenues go to the French Community.

In countries having mixed funding (licence fees and advertising) there has been a recent tendency towards eliminating advertising and, more generally, a growing dissatisfaction with the licence fee which often crops up in political debates (Italy, is a case in point, but criticism of the fee is recurrent also in Greece, Ireland, Germany, Switzerland, Poland and the Czech Republic).

France has seen a complicated process for the elimination of advertising public service television that is not yet complete.[24] The French PSB was funded through the licence fee and advertising up to 2009. In 2008, President Sarkozy announced his intention to eliminate commercial advertising as a means of funding for France Télévisions. The following year *Loi* n. 2009-258 of 5 March 2009 "*relative à la communication audiovisuelle et au nouveau service public de la télévision*" modified the 1986 law on the Freedom of Communication and started phasing-out advertising on the channels of France Télévisions (France 2, France 3, France 4 and France 5) with its elimination between eight in the evening and six in the morning from 5 January 2009[25] and ceasing advertising completely from 30 November 2011 (to coincide with the digital switchover). The political reasoning behind the law was twofold: on the one hand, the aim was to shift advertising resources from public to private TV; on the other hand (the only objective declared), was to raise the audience of the state channels. In just a few months

725 million for the BBC. The BBC estimates that at the end of 2021 the share of public funding will thus be reduced by 10% in real terms. Although the fee is the main source of funding for BBC, its commercial subsidiary BBC Worldwide contributed 20.5% of the total. It generated revenues of over GBP 1 billion and profits of GBP 133.8 million in 2015/2016 according to the BBC Worldwide Annual Review.

[24]The Government announced that a public consultation in October 2017 would gather comments from interested parties in order to simplify the rules for advertising on television.

[25]The legislation had a tricky passage through Parliament even before the law came into effect. In fact, President Sarkozy (through the Minister of Culture and Communication) asked the outgoing President of France Télévisions, Patrick de Carolis, to anticipate the application of the law by means of an extraordinary resolution of the Board of Directors (thus on 16 December 2008 the Board of Directors decided to abolish advertising between 20:00 and 06:00 on four of the group's five networks, with the exception of France O).

it became clear that both goals would be hard to achieve.[26] The law was strongly criticized, and its application hampered; in fact, in September 2010, the government was forced to establish a moratorium until January 2014, later extended by Parliament to January 2016.[27] The loss in revenue from the abolition of advertising was to be offset by new sources of public funding.

In Romania, the licence fee has been abolished since February 2017 with Law n. 1/2017 that amended the previous Law n. 41/94 on the Funding of Romanian radio stations.

Generally, the government is responsible for determining the licence fee, through the figure of the Minister for Communications, where this office exists, often together with the Minister of Economy and Finance. Frequently the annual cost of the fee is set by the government while the Parliament decides its appropriation in the Finance Law or in a specific source.[28] Only rarely is this task

[26] In fact, a paradoxical situation has occurred. Thanks also to the crisis, the estimates have proved inaccurate (of the €800 million of advertising, the lion's share—€480 million—would go to private national networks Tfl owned by Martin Bouygues, a personal friend of the President—and M6, of the German group Bertelsmann; €160 million to radio, print and billboard, €80 to the Internet and €80 on digital terrestrial channels). Furthermore, audience ratings on public networks have not increased.

[27] With the decision of 11 February 2010, the Council of State annulled the resolution of the Board of Directors on 16 December 2008 that had anticipated the abolition of advertising between 8 pm and 6 am. The clash between Government and Parliament was already apparent during the conversion process: the National Assembly, on 17 November 2010, approved an amendment against the Government's proposal, ruling in favour of maintaining advertising during the day; on the contrary, the Senate, on 4 December 2010, approved an amendment that provided for the complete abolition of advertising starting from 1 January 2016 (a choice then confirmed by the Joint Committee). Article 167 of Finance *Loi* n. 2010-1657 of 29 December 2010 again amended Art. 53, para. 6 of *Loi* 86-1067.

[28] There are many variables: the Ministry of Culture with the approval of Parliament's Finance Committee, in Denmark; the Ministry of Transport and Communications, in Finland. In France, Article 29 of Law 258/2009 amending Art. 1605 of the general tax code set a licence fee that is then indexed each year on the consumer price index (provided for in the economic, social and financial report annexed to the draft Finance Law). In Italy with Law 208/2015 (2016 Stability Law) the cost of the licence fee was set at €100. In the United Kingdom, the fee is negotiated with the Ministry of Culture, Sport and the Media for a six-year period but is deliberated annually by the Parliament in the Appropriation Act. In Sweden the cost of the licence fee value is decided every three years by Parliament on the basis of various inputs including: the Annual report provided by SVT; reports provided by academic experts on the needs of the public service broadcaster; Parliament's working groups dedicated to ensuring funding for the television broadcaster that must be adequate but not disproportionate (according to EU rules).

entrusted not to constitutional bodies but to independent authorities (e.g. *Kommission zur Ermittlung des Finanzbedarfs*—KEF—in Germany[29]); the Broadcasting Authority of Ireland and the National Broadcasting Council in Poland.[30]

The licence fee can be collected by specific Departments of the public broadcaster (e.g. Croatia, Norway, Slovenia, Slovakia, DR Licens OG Programservice, an Denmark in-house department of DR), by the Regulatory Authorities (FICORA in Finland, up to 2012, though its task was purely administrative because it was not competent to decide the sum of the funding nor how it would finance the activities of YLE), by subsidiary companies appointed to collect the fee (Ard Zdf *deutschlandradio beitragsservice* in Germany, *Radiotjänst i kiruna* in Sweden), by the Post Office (Ireland, Poland, Czech Republic), or by external companies.[31] Some countries have opted to collect the fee with the electricity or telephone bill (Italy since 2016, Greece, Portugal and Romania until its abolition in 2017).

[29] In Germany, the federal structure affects the structure of the funding system of PSB. The rate of the fee is established by the KEF, a Commission made up of 16 experts, through a complex procedure divided into three phases: (a) every 2 years the public state broadcasters notify the KEF of the estimated financial requirements; (b) the KEF verifies that they are in line with the principles of economic efficiency (Article 14 RstV) and makes a "recommendation" to the governments of the *Länder* about the level of the fee; and (c) the KEF determines the cost of the licence fee for the next period and proposes it to the *Länder*. Based on the inter-state agreement, the ultimate decision on the licence fee payable is up to the Parliaments of the *Länder* (Art. 7, para. 2 RfinStV). The Broadcasting Committee of the *Land* may disagree from the KEF proposal by advancing their reasoning. The new fee (*Rundfunkbeitrag*) was introduced on 1 January 2013. Germany was the first EU country to introduce a system for calculating the fee linked to residence (the so-called household charge). The reform was considered a success in generating more revenues for PSB, which allowed a reduction of the fee of EUR 17.50 per month from 1 April 2015. In April 2016, the KEF proposed a further decrease to EUR 17.20 monthly for the period 2017–2020, but in October 2016 was rejected by the *Länder* Government. The fee therefore remains unchanged at EUR 17.50 per month up to 2021.

[30] On 8 January 2016, an amendment to the Act on Radio and Television—a temporary solution awaiting an overall reform of PSB—has also regulated the public media financing system, modifying the licence fee rate.

[31] In Switzerland, in 2011 the Federal Council had entrusted the collection of the fee to the company Billag, a private company wholly owned by SWISSCOM, a Swiss telecommunications operator, 51% controlled by the state. Following a public tender, starting from 2019, Billag will be replaced by a private company called SERAFE to collect the property tax.

The basis on which the licence fee is charged varies; it ranges from the possession of one, or more than one, devices capable of receiving a broadcasting signal to the new devices on which broadcasts can be accessed such as a PC connected to the Internet or a mobile phone. In Switzerland, the 2015 Referendum confirmed the amendment to the Federal Law on Radio and Television (LRTV) to replace the former licence fee, based on possession of a radio or television, with an audiovisual licence fee now payable by all households and certain companies.[32] In Germany, the extension of the fee to devices other than radio and television, especially the PC (the so-called PC Tax) also passed through the Constitutional Court.[33]

In Denmark, the licence fee is determined by the possession of any type of device capable of receiving the television signal, for example, a PC connected to the Internet, mobile phones, etc. (see Law 477/2010, Part 10 dedicated to the licence fee). In the UK, from September 2016 the fee also covers all digital devices able to receive the BBC On Demand service called iPlayer; the licence fee must be paid by the owners of television sets, though there are a number of reductions or concessions for specific groups.

An analysis of the economic data of these countries makes it possible to highlight the proportion of revenue coming from the licence fee and that deriving from advertising: generally, public funding is greater, while revenues from advertising and other commercial resources are residual. In general, 78.4% of the income of the public service broadcasters in the EU countries comes from public resources. Advertising remains marginal at around 22%. In Italy and Ireland, however, for a certain period, the revenues from advertising almost equalled those from licence fees, though data from the

[32]For enterprises, the fee is based on turnover: companies with less than CHF 500,000 per year are exempt and account for around 75% of Swiss companies. This meant a reduction in the cost of the rent paid by residents: from CHF 462 to around CHF 400 per year.

[33]With the judgment of 30 January 2008, the Court rejected a petition of unconstitutionality of the application of the fee to the PCs and recognized the competence of the specialized Courts to rule for which devices the licence fee would be applicable (BvR 829/06). The early rulings of the state administrative Courts were conflicting: that of the Court of Wiesbaden of 19 November 2008 (case n. 5 K 243/08.WI) did not consider PCs as devices for receiving television signals while that of the Ausbach Court of 10 July 2008 (case n. AN 5 K 08.00348) believed that a PC capable of browsing is a device that allows the user to receive and watch TV programmes on the Internet.

EBU Funding of Public Service Media Report 2016 shows that income from advertising has since decreased in both countries. In four major markets such as France, Germany, Italy and the UK, the fee represents the main source of funding for PSB. In Eastern European countries the percentage of funding deriving from public subsidies is extremely high (in Bulgaria, for instance, almost 90%).

2. Among the countries that finance their PSB with public funds other than the licence fee are Spain, Belgium (not the French channels), the Netherlands, Portugal, Bulgaria, Lithuania and Latvia. The experiences of these different countries vary, and they can only be grouped into a single class with rather vague outlines. Here too, public funding is accompanied by revenue from advertising and other commercial sources.

   In Belgium, decrees implemented at the end of the 1990s replaced the fee with public funding as established in the five-year contracts stipulated between the Governments of the Communities and their public broadcasters. Certain scholars have criticized the use of contracts to decide on funding; while the law requires a more complex process (and also involves minorities), the contract is not considered sufficiently transparent because it is stipulated between a Ministry and the broadcaster (Coppens and Frieda 2006). In addition to advertising, most of the funding is given by the government grant, granted on the basis of the service obligations imposed on the public service broadcasters and various performance criteria to be achieved in the period established beforehand. Advertising (in various forms) is allowed at a rate of revenue lower than the grant. In the Netherlands the fee has been replaced by direct funding since 2000; it is flanked by advertising and other forms of funding deriving from "self-generated" funds (namely activities such as the publication of television programme guides, sponsorships, intellectual property rights, etc.).[34] In Finland, the new tax applies to private individuals and commercial enterprises but is no longer based on the possession of a television set. The tax is inspired by the principle that PSB is aimed at all Finns, guaranteed through TV, radio,

[34] Public funding 68%—Advertising 23%—Other commercial activities 3%—Other revenue 6%.

Internet and accessible through different devices.[35] In Portugal, Article 1 of *Lei* n. 30/2003, of 22 August on the "Financiamento do Serviço Público de Rádio e de Televisão" (as amended by the *Decretos-Leis* 169A/2005; 230/2007 e 107/2010), established public funding of Portuguese broadcasting in two different ways: "cobrança da contribuição para o áudio-visual" (for radio) and "indemnizações compensatórias e [...] receita da contribuição" (for television). This is a state contribution directly attributable to broadcasting services which, pursuant to Article 3, para. 2 "incide sobre o fornecimento de energia eléctrica, sendo devida mensalmente pelos respectivos consumidores." Law 7-A/2016 of 30/3/2016 reformed Articles 4 and 6 of Law n. 30 of 2003 regarding the contribution to be paid in some countries, such as in Bulgaria,[36] Latvia[37] and Lithuania.[38]

In Spain, RTVE has always been financed with a public contribution alongside other commercial resources (such as the sale of programmes). Law 8/2009 of 28 August on the "Financiación de la Corporación de Radio y Televisión Española" adopted by Royal

[35]The tax is levied by the Finnish revenue agency then transferred to the State Fund for Radio and TV and finally turned over to YLE after deducting the VAT. The rate of the tax is frozen until 2019 is calculated on 0.68% of income and must not exceed €140.

[36]Ex Art. 70 L. 138/24 of 1998, the loan is made up as follows: (1) a special broadcasting fund in which the fees paid by the citizens are added to the electricity bill; (2) subsidies from the state budget; (3) revenues from commercial activities and sponsorships; (4) additional revenues related to additional broadcasting activities; (5) donations and legacies; and (6) interest and other revenues related to radio and television activities and of a private nature.

[37]The mass media Law of 2010 provides the following sources of funding (Article 70): state subsidy; revenues from economic activities; donations from natural and legal persons, including foreigners; other forms of funding provided for in regulatory agreements. In addition, there is advertising with some restrictions.

[38]Law I-1571 of 1996 envisaged a licence fee, but this method of funding has never been fully implemented because of the annual revisions that altered the part concerning funding. The Law of 22 December 2005 provides for a new system of mixed funding composed of various sources (Article 15): a "subsidy" coming out of the state budget (the amount of which is decided annually by the Parliament); publishing and programming activities; sponsorships; commercial and economic activities; advertising (with some limitations). The proportion of public funding is the most significant: 90.6%—Commercial 9.3%—Other sources 0.1%.

Decree 1004/2010, abolished advertising. This legislation is part of an overall plan for the renewal of PSB, undertaken under Law 17/2006 and continued with Law 7/2010 to guarantee its independence from both a structural and an economic point of view (see Chapter 6). The earlier mixed funding system had caused the collapse of RTVE and many regional broadcasters, despite subsidies from the respective Autonomous Communities. The state authorized RTVE to issue a certain amount of public debt in the form of 5-year bonds with unlimited guarantees by the state itself. These bonds were bought by investors, but they had to be repaid by RTVE, together with interest. This mechanism led to an increase in the indebtedness of RTVE and some regional TVs, leading to their closure. The 2009 reform aimed to remedy the indebtedness of public service broadcasters, without restoring the clumsy and unpopular licence fee that had been abolished many years earlier. The law eliminated advertising but permitted sponsorships of cultural and sporting programmes suited to the remit of RTVE's public service mission, in order to reduce costs (first transitional provision). The new funding system is complex and includes: state subsidies; different types of taxes ranging from fees for the fulfilment of public service obligations and burdening directly on the state budget, to new or renewed forms of taxation, such as that on the use of the airwaves and on telecommunications operators and the contribution of commercial broadcasters (Article 2).

Conclusion

This chapter described the legal framework of all the EU countries in an analytical-comparative analysis and focussed on two important issues to evaluate the independence and pluralism of the public broadcasters (decentralized organization of the broadcaster and method of funding).

The decentralization of the public broadcasters indicates a respect for certain values ascribed to a public service such as the promotion of local culture, the protection of ethnic and linguistic minorities and, more generally, of regional identities. The analysis shows that the regional TVs are subject to the internal dynamics and the centrifugal or centripetal thrusts that characterize the territorial form of the state (centralized or decentralized). However, classifications based exclusively on normative parameters linked to the territorial form of state prove insufficient to test the real degree of decentralization of PSB. To appreciate the actual degree of "proximity" of a public broadcaster to a territorial collectivity, further criteria were used such as television "production," or a combination of legal and extralegal parameters.

The method of funding reflects the relations between the state and the society, culture and market of a country and is closely linked to the role of PSB as a medium of communication and influencer of public opinion.

The existing wide range of solutions offers interesting insights for comparison that, starting from the data on the internal organization of the public broadcasters of the EU member states (composition of the bodies, appointment procedure, term of office, etc.) leads to considerations on the way they operate and their relationship with state and local political institutions, namely, their governance.

The cross-sectional and comparative analysis of legislation on the organization of PSB could constitute a base of useful information for studies in other disciplines (communication sciences, communication sociology, political science, with emphasis on public communication, etc.) that will perforce consider the normative framework.

However, the normative framework alone can be misleading for the overall analysis if it is not contextualized in the broader scenario of the political and institutional environment of a country since it may provide a limited (and sometimes mistaken) view of the governance of public broadcasters.

References

Carleton Greene, H. (1969). *The third floor front: A view of broadcasting in the sixties*. London: University of Michigan.

Coppens, T., & Frieda, S. (2006). Enforcing performance: New approaches to govern public service broadcasting. *Media, Culture and Society, 28*(2), 261–284.

Debbasch, C. (1969). *Le droit de la radio et de la télévision*. Paris: PUF.

European Audiovisual Observatory. (2016). *Iris special: Regional and local broadcasting in Europe*. Strasbourg: European Audiovisual Observatory.

Garitaonandía, C. (1993). Regional television in Europe. *European Journal of Communication, 8*, 277–294.

Garitaonandía, C. (2000). *El mosaico audiovisual: las televisiones regionales en Europa*. In M. T. Aubach Guiu & M. Rubio Lacoba (Coord.), *Comunicación audiovisual y desarrollo de las regiones. Actas del II congreso internacional,*

Salamanca del 28 al 30 de noviembre de 1996. Salamanca: Universidad Pontificia de Salamanca.

Garitaonandía, C., & Moragas, M. (1995). *Decentralization in the global era*. New Barnet: Herts.

Konijnenbelt, W. (1994). Discours de la methode en droit public comparé. In K. Baele-Woelki, F. W. Grosheide, E. H. Hondius, & G. J. W. Steenhoff (Eds.), *Comparability and Evaluation*. Norwell: Martinus Nijhoff Publishers.

McDonnell, J. (1987). Public broadcasting: Cultural goods or commercial commodity. *Communication Research Trends, 8*(3–4), 13.

Morawski, P. (2005). Presentazione. In G. Richeri (Ed.), *Le televisioni pubbliche nelle regioni d'Europa*. Roma: Rai-Eri.

Musso, P. (1991). *Régions d'Europe et télévision*. Nord Pas de Calais: Editions Miroirs.

Nikolova, R. (2016). On-budget subsidies for public media. *IRIS* 2016-3/6.

Richeri, G. (Ed.). (2005). *Le televisioni pubbliche nelle regioni d'Europa*. Roma: Rai-Eri.

Rosado Iglesias, G. (1998). La regionalizzazione del sistema televisivo nell'esperienza comparata. In T. Groppi (Ed.), *Principio di autonomia e forma di stato. La partecipazione delle collettività territoriali alle funzioni dello Stato centrale nella prospettiva comparata*. Torino: Giappichelli.

Smith, A. (Ed.). (1995). *Television: An international history*. Oxford and New York: Oxford University Press.

Stephane, R. (1983). *Première Conference des télévision regionales*. Lille: CIRCOM.

Vandelli, L. (2017). Presentación. In G. Pavani & L. Estupiñan Achury (Eds.), *Plurinacionalismo y centralismo. Tensiones del Estado unitario en América latina*. Bogotà: Universidad Libre de Colombia.

Zimmerman, P. (1990). Las televisiones regionales en Europa. In RTVV (Ed.), *Las radiotelevisiones en el espacio europeo*. Valencia: RTTV.

CHAPTER 6

The Appointment Processes of the Management Bodies

Abstract This chapter analyses data on the structure of public service broadcasters to pinpoint the dynamics of the appointment process of public broadcasters' managing bodies and to offer a more realistic analysis of parliamentary appointments. The examination of legislation provides some initial data, however, the normative framework alone, if not contextualized in the broader scenario of the political-institutional environment of a country, can be misleading for the overall analysis, since it may provide a limited (and sometimes mistaken) view of the governance of public broadcasters. The author interprets the normative framework by viewing it through the form of government adopted, and how it developed diversely over time in certain emblematic countries (three of them with parliamentary government: the UK, Italy and Spain, and one with a form of semi-presidential government).

Keywords Public service broadcasters · Form of government
Management bodies · Governance · Political parties

Introduction

A common trend emerges from the comparative framework outlined in the previous chapter: Parliament almost always intervenes in the appointment of the members of the collegial body of the public broadcaster

G. Pavani, *The Structure and Governance of Public Service Broadcasting*, https://doi.org/10.1007/978-3-319-96731-8_6

(Board) though rarely alone, more often doing so together with other institutional bodies (in particular the government and independent Authorities). Furthermore, there is a growing tendency to involve employee representatives and/or civil society. However, this will be no more than a starting point, as normative data when considered alone cannot suffice to fully comprehend the actual functioning of the appointment process. Indeed, it would be simplistic to say that the parliamentary appointment of the collegial Board provides an absolute guarantee of the latter's independence, while government intervention clearly indicates that the Board's members will be politicized.

This chapter analyses data relating to how internal bodies are appointed in order to pinpoint the dynamics of the appointment process of public broadcasters' managing bodies and to offer a more realistic analysis of parliamentary appointments.

Rethinking a Common Trend

In the television sector, adopting a prototype (*tertium comparationis*) independent body built on the stringent, classical criteria (linked the designation of the advisory and executive board, the term of office, the incompatibility and certain subjective and professional requirements of members) applied almost automatically to a range of public institutions, cannot rightly be used as a point of comparison.

The situation appears even more complex as we are dealing with an organization at the service of a fundamental freedom that has always been closely connected with a country's political expression. Hence, it is obvious that the legal categories used to test the degree of independence of some institutions/public entities and/or independent administrative authorities cannot be seamlessly applied to the PSB. Any attempt to do so would be to ignore the special mission of broadcasters and their link to the fundamental freedom of expression and the inevitable two-way relationship with the political system under which they operate (PSB is also a mouthpiece for political groups as well as being in part unavoidably influenced by them).

With this in mind, it is clear that unless contextualized in the broader scenario of the political-institutional environment of a country, normative data considered alone may be misleading for an overall analysis, providing a limited (and sometimes mistaken) view of the structure and governance of PSB.

I will firstly attempt to prove this assumption empirically by using a legal instrument, i.e. the form of government, understood in the broadest sense, and including all the variables that are essential to it: the political-party system and electoral formula. I will try to interpret the normative data through the lens of the form of government adopted, bearing in mind its varied development over time in different Countries. I will describe the normative profiles of three legal systems with a parliamentary system (Italy, United Kingdom and Spain) and one with a semi-presidential system (France).

Italy

In Italy, television currently remains by far the most common source of information: "76% of citizens obtain information through free TV, 44% through newspapers, 11% through pay TV."[1] Television continues to dominate over the Internet as a channel of information, although the number of Italians who choose the Internet to access information daily is growing, and the access to the Internet is becoming increasingly important for the implementation of fundamental rights (Frosini 2015).

The setting up of RAI-Radio Audizioni Italia with Decree 457/1944 marked the birth of Italian PSB. Radio Audizioni Italia was founded to replace the company that had previously enjoyed a monopoly on broadcasting (the Unione Radiofonica Italiana, founded in 1924, later to become EIAR in 1927). In 1952, the company became RAI-Radiotelevisione Italiana and was granted exclusive broadcasting rights for 20 years. The RAI is a state-owned private company and its activities are classed as essential public services. Ex Article 2, para. 1, letter t), of Legislative Decree n. 177 of 2005, amended in 2010 defines "public service broadcasting" as "the exercise of public service by concession in the broadcasting sector through the overall programming, not only of information services, by the concessionary company" (for a comment on the decree see Zeno-Zencovich 2010).

Like other European countries, Italy's broadcasting system was determined by both political and economic decisions (Gardini 2007). However, the Italian system possesses certain unique features that may be considered anomalies by some: the way in which the Italian

[1] Data from dossier S. 1880 of the legislative procedure of "Riforma della RAI e del servizio pubblico radiotelevisivo."

broadcasting system developed; the mismatch between Italy's system as a regionalized unitary state and the weak decentralised organisation of PSB; the Parliamentary Supervisory Committee on RAI; and the relationship between the Company and the country's political class (Pavani 2017, p. 508*ff.*).

The first anomaly concerns the way in which the Italian broadcasting system grew. A variety of factors may explain this anomaly. Firstly, legislation was slow (serving only to recognize existing situations without altering them), and sometimes lacking (enabling private companies to broadcast without authorization and the PSB to compete with a single competitor). Secondly, the Italian Constitutional Court advanced the development of the broadcasting system through a series of judgments, thus playing a para-legislative role. The Court intervened in order to implement the exercise of freedom of expression, the "cornerstone of democratic order" (Italian Constitutional Court, judgment 84/1969).

Thus, from its earliest judgment on state monopoly (59/1960) and during the so called "caos dell'etere" in the 1970s (judgment 225/1974), in the period where a single business group had risen to dominate,[2] until the so-called "Mammì law" (Law 223/1990 on the "Regulation of the public and private broadcasting system"), which recognised and legitimised the legislative duopoly of Fininvest-Rai, the Constitutional Court laid the foundations of the broadcasting system (Chapter 4).

In exercising its quasi-legislative task, the Constitutional Court was guided by a basic principle of democracy: the principle of pluralism, considered as both internal, external and substantial. Examples of such intervention are Judgment n. 420/1994 that indicated a percentage

[2]It is well known that in 1980 Silvio Berlusconi created the Canale 5 network offering the same programming nationwide by using a technique that enabled broadcasting the same programme at the same time in different areas of the territory, that were hence limited areas. Certain strategic choices of television programming (the soap opera Dallas and the 1980 Mundialito) consolidated the network and enabled it to buy others (Italia 1 and Rete 4).

To remedy this situation in 1984 then Prime Minister Bettino Craxi, signed two Decree Laws to enable the business group to maintain control of the three broadcasters. Political tension was high: the first decree law was blocked by Parliament, the latter was converted to Law 10/1985, with which the Socialist Party granted a mini-reform of the RAI enabling appointment the of all sixteen members of the Board of directors to the Supervisory Committee.

threshold to ensure broadcasting pluralism in proportion to the number of national networks, and Judgment n. 466/2002, in which the Court set a deadline for the conclusion of the transitional period envisaged in Law 249/1997 ("Maccanico Law") on the "Establishment of the Communications Authority and regulations governing telecommunications and broadcasting systems" (AGCOM).

In 2004, a Law taking the name of the then Minister of Communications Gasparri (Law 112/2004 on "Regulations and principles governing the set-up of the broadcasting system and the RAI-Radiotelevisione italiana S.p.a., authorizing the government to issue a consolidated broadcasting act") was approved during the second Berlusconi Government.[3] This Law was later transposed (without significant changes) in the Consolidated Broadcasting Code (Legislative Decree 177/2005 "*Testo Unico dei servizi di media audiovisivi e radiofonici* – TUSMAR") that now constitutes the main legal reference as regards broadcasting.

Another particularly Italian anomaly that hung like a shadow over Italy for almost two decades was the issue of the conflict of interests posed by the rise to political power of Silvio Berlusconi. Over a period of nearly twenty years, though not continuously, a single individual (Berlusconi), held the position of Prime Minister while remaining the controlling shareholder of the country's major commercial television company, Mediaset. While this issue more closely concerns concentration of media ownership than the independence of the organs of the public broadcaster, the two topics overlap. Essentially, Italy saw a coincidence of economic interests and government functions that has occurred in no other part of the comparative landscape.

Clearly, Italian political history has impacted strongly on the television system and, in particular, on RAI. The second anomaly concerns the role of the Parliamentary Supervisory Committee of RAI on the appointment of the top management of the public broadcaster.

[3]The law was passed with 142 votes in favour, 91 against and 1 abstention; it passed the six stages between the Chamber of Deputies and Senate, during which more than 14,000 amendments and a presidential veto were filed. The President of the Republic Carlo Azeglio Ciampi sent the bill back to Parliament for violation of the principle of pluralism of information and called on the Parliament to comply with the directions given by the Constitutional Court over the years and to apply them to the new technological scenario of digital broadcasts.

The relationship between the political parties and PSB gave rise to a system referred to as 'lottizzazione' (literally, parcelling out). In practice, this entailed the division and allocation of the key positions of RAI (Board members and Chair) being the prerogative of the government from the post-war period to the 1970s, and later of the parliamentary groups that make up the bicameral Parliamentary Committee "for the general guidance and supervision of broadcasting services" (*Commissione di Vigilanza RAI*), hereafter the Supervisory Committee. This practice reflects closely the political history of the country, marked by a large number of political parties and the anomaly of having a Parliamentary Supervisory Committee that both appoints the top executives of RAI while also monitoring its operations.

The system of parliamentary government, together with an electoral system that for a long time was proportional in nature, and the plethora of political parties represented in Parliament (and also in the governments dominated by the Christian Democrats)[4] led to the three RAI channels being shared out, whereby they were "influenced" respectively by the Christian Democrats (RAI 1), the Socialist Party (RAI 2) and the Communist Party (RAI 3).

Law n. 103/1975, in line with developments in other countries, shifted the control of PSB from the government to parliament in order to include minorities when making strategic decisions related to radio and TV broadcasting. This was precisely the objective of the Supervisory Committee, established on the basis of information provided by the Constitutional Court.

The Supervisory Committee participated in the appointment of members of RAI's Board and its Chair; it has responsibility in matters regarding the steering of RAI, supervision, ensuring access to public broadcasting by collective bodies that bear socially relevant interests, public communication and equal access during election and referendum campaigns (together with AGCOM). The Supervisory Committee thus

[4] Political and cultural-religious (Catholic) aspects were interweaved in the development of the Italian party system and have had indirect effects on RAI, both at the structural and organisational level (the influence of the DC diminished but did not disappear with the passage from government appointments to parliamentary appointments of the Supervisory Committee; thus, the dissolution of the DC only produced a distribution of the Catholic grouping among the various streams of new or old parties), and at the practical level of programming content.

has the power to give RAI "guidance codes" related to the criteria and content of radio and television programming, while respecting the independence of journalists and the autonomy that should characterise the directors of the public service.

The composition of the Supervisory Committee, which proportionately reflects the political movements represented in Parliament, should ensure respect for the pluralism of the programming of the PSB concessionary.

However, a strong political and cultural (and indeed religious) influence on RAI remains a constant of the Italian system.

The (substantial) changes in the form of government of the 1990s, produced by the shift from a proportional electoral system to a predominantly majoritarian system, forced the parties to coalesce into two poles: the centre-right and centre-left. This led to a previously unseen governmental stability but served only to change the balance within the Supervisory Committee, without eliminating the practice of sharing out the spoils. Indeed, with the current electoral system, many political forces remain outside Parliament and therefore do not participate in decisions on PSB. As noted by both scholars engaged in studying the sociology of communication and political science, the participation of political parties (in an abstract sense, of all the political parties) is an embodiment of pluralism. However, when the practice of allocation is the prerogative of the few political parties that make up the government majority, pluralism is sacrificed, and parliamentary opposition remains totally excluded.

Until the existence of Law 220/2015, the rules on the composition of the Board and the appointment of the Chair regulated the in-progress situation associated with the privatisation procedure of the body; a situation that never reached completion.

Article 49 of the TUSMAR stipulated that the nine Board members were to be appointed by the Assembly; the Chair of the Board was to be appointed by the Board from among its members, with the approval of the Supervisory Committee (with a 2/3 majority); the Director-General was appointed by the Board, in agreement with the Assembly. This organisational system should have been subject to the full privatisation of RAI, which was to come about in a series of stages (linked to the progressive transfer of the capital), each of which provided for a different system of appointments.

Hence, through all these years, the rules of the TUSMAR were not applied and members of the Board were chosen by the Supervisory Committee (7 members, expressed by a majority) and the Minister of Economy (2 members, including the Chair, with the consent of 2/3 of the Committee).

This situation of stagnation has partly been resolved by Law 220/2015, presented by the Minister for Economic Development to the Senate on April 20, 2015, which was approved on December 22, 2015 and entered into force on January 30, 2016.

Despite the title of the law ("Reform of the RAI and of public service broadcasting") this law, in fact, only partially reforms the broadcasting system.

The intervention on the governance of RAI is equally weak, with the only change regarding the procedures for designating top executives. Until 10% of the capital is sold off (Article 21 of Law n. 112/2004) the innovations are as follows:

- a reduction in the numbers of members on the Board from 9 to 7, of which: 2 are elected by the Chamber of Deputies and 2 by the Senate, with voting limited to a single candidate (after submission of the application and publication of curricula on the Internet); 2 appointed by the government and 1 appointed by an Assembly of the company's employees who have held a contract of employment for at least three consecutive years. The law defines a number of causes that exclude the possibility of candidacy or election but does not specifically define the requirements of Board members (Article 2, para. 1 refers only to "elevated professionalism and proven experience in the legal, financial, industrial and cultural sectors."). The members may be dismissed with a resolution of the Assembly, only after an assessment by the Supervisory Committee. The Board, in addition to the duties assigned by law and the statutes of the company, approves the business plan and the editorial plan, the estimate of annual expenditure, as well as investments that exceed 10 million Euro, partly as they cover several years.
- appointment of the Chair by the Board from among its members, subject to approval of 2/3 of the members of the Supervisory Committee. The Chair can be entrusted with powers in the fields of external and institutional relations and supervision of internal

auditing control, after the shareholders' resolution authorising such delegation.

- introduction of the figure of the CEO (in place of the Director General) to be appointed by the Board at the proposal of the shareholders' assembly (currently controlled almost entirely by the Ministry of Economy and Finance, with SIAE- the Italian Society of Authors and Publishers, holding a little less than 1%). The CEO will have a three-year mandate and greater decision-making powers with respect to the previous figure of the Director General, especially regarding the appointment of network managers, editors in chief and some groups of executives (the CEO cannot be a RAI employee: in this case he/she must resign or seek leave).

The Supervisory Committee loses those duties that interfere with the management of the company and its governance. However, it maintains its functions related to outlining the overall guidelines and supervising the PSB, while the Council of Ministers will have greater powers to influence the guidelines for the renewal of the service contract (which rises from 3 to 5 years), hitherto defined by the Supervisory Committee and the Ministry of Economic Development.

The reform falls within the framework of the previous legislation; specifically, the law does not touch on any of the major issues that a reform of the broadcasting system should now regulate and ignores developments in the areas of broadcasting that have changed dramatically since the 2004 legislation.

No political or strategic decision, which might affect the nature of the service, either subjectively or objectively, emerges for the public broadcaster. Its structure (which is formally decentralized, with weak regional departments, remains unchanged except for a level of greater autonomy granted to Regions with special status). Nor is the repeated and, in fact, in-house concession of the public service to RAI questioned, although many consider that RAI has failed to fulfil its public service mission and the general economic interest (Gardini 2008, p. 663*ff.*).

The intervention on the governance of RAI is equally weak, with the only change regarding the procedures for designating top executives.

Immediately after its presentation in the Senate, the reform Bill suffered a setback; the Senate Budget Service had noted that in some key steps the Bill contained no more than a "mere statement of the thematic areas to be addressed", without explicitly indicating the "procedures or strategies to be activated" for the pursuit of its declared goals. Moreover, the technical report accompanying the Bill did "not present data relating to important parameters" for the assessment of the actual effectiveness of the measure. In particular, "blank proxies" that entrusted the future regulation of the public funding and the regulatory reorganization of the state broadcaster to the government were sanctioned.

Similar criticism was expressed by many scholars, even during parliamentary hearings.[5]

The reform remains incomplete because the Government decrees for its implementation were never approved and the delegation expired.

The anomalies of the Italian broadcasting system are thus confirmed. Furthermore, the (rather strong) link between the public broadcaster and the political forces seems unlikely to disappear with the new Law 220/2015.

Nonetheless, the concept of anomaly is undoubtedly relative: it can be defined only through comparison between experiences that have homogeneous elements. Such must be the approach when evaluating the anomalies of the Italian broadcasting system.

The spread of private radio and television before the fall of the monopoly and the advent of a public-private duopoly system has no equal in the comparative panorama. The unresolved problem of the conflict of interest that has characterised Italy for a long time is also anomalous. Equally anomalous or, at least not in line with some of the experiences of decentralized states, is the fact that the RAI's organisation is only formally decentralized (see Chapter 5).

The tendency for regulation and state intervention in the communications sector and, particularly, in the broadcasting sector is less anomalous. This tendency is not in line with the indications of the European Union that encourage light-touch regulation of the media and self-regulatory or co-regulatory practices (from the Directives on electronic communications of 2002 to Directive 2010/13/EU). On the other hand, the active and sometimes alternative role played by the Constitutional Court can be clearly considered anomalous.

[5] See, the hearings in front of the plenary Commissions VII and IX of the Chamber of Deputies of Professor Roberto Zaccaria, former Chairman of the RAI of 29 September 2015 representing the "Associazione Art. 21".

The United Kingdom

In 1922 the British Broadcasting Company, established by the Post Office as a cooperative venture owned by the radio industry, started daily transmissions as the sole licensed radio broadcaster. The company was restructured in 1927 into the British Broadcasting Corporation, the present-day BBC (Humphreys 1996, p. 112).

Over the years, many Committees have discussed changes to governance, financing arrangements and the role and remit of the BBC, with a view to ensuring the independence of PSB (Chapter 2).

The British experience is, on the one hand, an example of a connection between public service broadcasting and the Executive, but at the same time an example of independence, especially as far as the provision of information is concerned.

In fact, the BBC is not regulated by an Act of Parliament but by a Royal Charter, issued in the exercise of the Crown Prerogative powers (nominally exercised by the Monarch, but in practice governmental) and adopted by Order in Council and by an Agreement that is adopted by a government act. Moreover, the (first) appointment of Governors and (later) the BBC Trust is (formally) an Act of the Monarch, but actually governmental (the members are officially appointed by the Queen following their selection by the Prime Minister, subject to approval by the Department of Culture, Media and Sport).

The vulnerability of the BBC's existence caused by the chosen source raised much debate and various alternative solutions were proposed but never adopted (Barendt 1994, p. 20*f.*).

Despite the absence of formal guarantees for the public broadcaster and, more generally, for the freedom of expression (due to the fact that the British Constitution is not contained in a formal written document), independence has always been a supreme value for the British broadcaster who has pursued and protected this feature "through a system of mutual expectations and cultural norms and this has meant that [...] there has been a reluctance to use them to the full for political advantage" (Prosser 2007, p. 112), although some would argue there has been a certain lack of diversity in appointments and a parsimonious application of "the great and the good"[6] as a criterion for selection.

[6] See Prosser (2007, p. 112). Again, the adoption of the Human Rights Act 1998 affects another piece of the vast British mosaic of sources (and culture), converting disputes on what were political issues into legal disputes.

The requirement of independence is pursued both from a "subjective" point of view of (members of the managing bodies are appointed in accordance with the so-called Nolan Principles, seven principles established by the Committee on Standards in Public Life, during the presidency of Lord Nolan) and from a structural one.

The Corporation's governance has been subject to various changes, especially in the last two renewals of the Royal Charter.

In the past, there have been various interpretations of the role of the Governors, especially regarding that of the Director-General. The Board of Governors was composed of 12 members (the number changed several times with the various Royal Charters), of which 4 represented the interests of the Nations, and the Director-General was appointed from among these. This body was responsible for establishing guidelines and deciding the policies of the British public broadcaster, known to hold its independence as a defining characteristic.

Usually, the Governors went no further than providing a basic orientation of the BBC mandate and abstained from any practical management of the body, leaving this task to the Director-General and senior managers (thus, any issues raised with the Governors had, in fact, already been decided by members of the executive) (Munro 1979, pp. 18–19).

For some time, there had been clamour for change; in 2005, the Green Paper of the Department for Culture, Media, Sport, entitled "A strong BBC, Independent of Government" proposed the replacement of the Board of Governors, after eighty years of service (with the BBC Trust) and the creation of a new executive body (Executive Board). These changes were incorporated into the 2007 Royal Charter, which established a dual organization of the BBC, with two collegial bodies: the Trust (general oversight and strategic direction) and the Executive Board (management) (Article 9).

The BBC Trust consisted of a Chair, a Vice-Chairperson, and a minimum number of ten Trustees, four of whom represented the Home Nations (England, Wales, Scotland and Northern Ireland).

The 2007 Royal Charter established that "The Queen, on advice from government ministers and an independent commissioner for public appointments, appoints its 12 trustees." The composition of the Trust was thus identical to that of the Board of Governors, yet there was a change in the selection process of its members, which became more transparent and participative with the involvement of the Office of the Commissioner for Public Appointments.

The appointment process, however, remained (formally) in the hands of the Queen, but (in practice) was decided by the government. The mandate was 5 years, with the possibility for members to be re-elected.

The BBC Trust chose the Chair who could also be the BBC's Director-General (Executive Director and in charge of the Corporation's editorial choices). In this case, the Chair exercised a significant influence on the Commission responsible for electing members of the Executive Board. This collegiate body included both "executive members" and "non-executive members," for a total of 12 members.

The term of office of the Executive Board was determined at the time of appointment, although in principle it was the same as that of the Trust members, i.e. 5 years.

The Trust had the function of setting the BBC's overall strategy and setting and assessing the performance of the Executive Board. We recall that the BBC "(...) exists to create public value" and "(...) public value should be the goal for everything BBC does" (BBC 2004, pp. 7, 10).

The implementation and specification of the Public Purposes laid down by the Royal Charter was therefore the responsibility of the Trust, which was to ensure that the activities of the BBC fell within the broader concept of upholding public value, a principle widely studied in Anglo-Saxon theory of public management (see, at least, Moore 1995; Kelly et al. 2002).

The choice that clearly emerges from the 2007 Royal Charter to create "public value by serving people both as individuals and as citizens" through digital innovation, invested the Trust's most important mission, namely to contribute to democracy and culture by "helping to create a more informed society based on shared understanding" (BBC 2004).

Some of the Trust's functions, however, overlapped with those of the Executive Board and OFCOM, and added functions of regulation to those of supervision, thereby undermining its role of upholding the public interest and the interests of users.[7]

[7]From a procedural point of view, in order to fulfill this mission, the Trust was responsible for carrying out the public value test (PVT), an *ex ante* test conducted to decide whether to insert a new service in the public service basket and it had full discretion on the so-called significance test (Donders and Pauwels 2010, pp. 133–148). The PVT is not characteristic of the British system (v. Moe 2010, pp. 207–223) and pertains to the culture of public value (Jakubowicz 2007, pp. 29–50; Muñoz Saldaña 2008, pp. 203–219), however, the British experience is turning into a model to imitate.

This organization was strongly criticized for the appointment process for members of the BBC Trust and the division between executive and non-executive members of the BBC Executive Board, inducing some that said, “it is clear that the reforms introduced by the new Charter are only a half measure, leaving many pressing issues untouched” (Katsirea 2008, p. 128).

To improve relations between the two bodies, as early as 2013 it was proposed that the Trust publish the objectives and priorities it would set to the Board, which would report to the trustee throughout the year through quarterly business updates, opinions, and an “Exceptional Business Report” if the implementation of a project were at risk (BBC 2013).

The 2017 Royal Charter modified the BBC’s organizational structure once again. The preparatory work, as usual, was laid down in a White Paper (“A BBC for the Future: a Broadcaster of Distinction”, Department for Digital, Culture Media & Sport, 2016), accompanied by an independent study on governance and regulation by the British Conservative Government (Sir David Clementi, A Review of the Governance and Regulation of the BBC, Department of Culture Media & Sport, March 2016). These studies recommended an organizational change to remedy excessive confusion between managerial and regulatory roles. The alternative proposals were: the creation of a new, special, regulator (OfBeeb) that would work alongside the existing (OFCOM) Authority or broadening OFCOM’s remit to the overall regulation of the BBC. The latter option was chosen, thus avoiding two-track regulation while ensuring the separation of governance functions from those of regulation by clearly identifying the responsible parties.

The new structure provides for a single Board which, acting collectively, is responsible for the proper, effective and independent exercise of all the functions of the BBC in accordance with the provisions set out in this Charter and the Framework Agreement (Article 19 (1)).

The Board must consist of a number of non-executive members (including the Chair) and a number of executive members. The total number of members must be 14 (Article 21 (1)).

In addition to the Chair, the non-executive members are the four Nation Members and five other members. The executive members of the Board must be the Director General and three other members (Article 21 (3)).

Only the Chair and the four Nation Members are appointed by Order in Council through a public process that should guarantee the principle of trasparency. The Commissioner for Public Appointments will ensure that the appointment is made in accordance with the Governance Code (Article 22 (3)).

The remaining executive and non-executive members of the Board are selected by a Nominations Committee of the Board itself (Article 31). This does away with the governmental appointment system that characterized both the Governors and the Trust. The earliest comments do not recognize any revolutionary objectives in this reform: "the threats to the BBC's status as a major public service broadcaster have not gone away. They have only been downgraded" (Freedman 2016).

Thus, the appointment of the executive body of the BBC has passed from the Executive Board, appointed indirectly by the government through the Trust (in turn, in practice appointed by the government) to a (single) Board of which less than half—the most "important" part—is appointed directly by the government, through a transparent, selective procedure.

Over time, while there was a rising potential for interference on the public broadcaster by the governmental group in office, further strengthened by a shift towards a form of government that enhances the Executive and endows it with a wider range of instruments in routine matters, there was a prevailing conception of the public broadcaster formed on historical and cultural factors that act as regulatory antibodies. However, there has been criticism over the years.[8]

The singularity of the British model should therefore be sought in the history and culture of the country, which are reflected in its broadcasting service. This culture has allowed the public broadcaster to remain an independent body, external to political shifts and changes in government (Morgan 1986).

These features seem to hold, despite the changes in the British political and party landscape of the last few years that have shifted from a

[8]Certain episodes of indirect political influence have left their mark in the long history of the BBC: the resignation of the Director-General Alasdair Milne from the Board of Governors, under pressure from Margaret Thatcher, or the more recent Kelly affair related to news reporting on the war in Iraq that led to the resignation of Greg Dyke. See, on this subject, Barnett (2005, p. 330*ff.*).

bipartisan system (with two major opposing parties that alternated in the country's leadership) to a more unstable system with less clearly distinct election results compared to the past.

Spain

Democratic development of the Spanish Radio and Television services has a very recent history. In fact, until the death of Franco in 1975 and the approval of the Constitution three years later, all the media were used to further the objectives of the regime.

State radio and television were combined into a single *servicio público centralizado* called *Radio y Televisión Española* (RTVE) in 1973. The Ministry of Information and Tourism remained at the head of this—formally autonomous—body meaning the controlling and controlled party were one and the same (the Director General of RTVE was the head of the Ministry).

The 1978 Democratic Constitution set the stage for change, even though it did not make any explicit reference to PSB. Article 20 recognizes freedom of expression "through any media of diffusion" and refers to the legislator for the regulation and control of the media of social communication, which must guarantee access to "significant social and political groups, respecting the pluralism of society and the different languages of Spain" (Article 20.3).

PSB in the new democratic Spain was regulated for the first time in 1980 with *Ley* 4/1980—*Estatuto de la Radio y la Televisión*—that entered into force in 1982 and considered radio and television broadcasting as "essential public services," subject to the control of the parliamentary committee (the 12 members of the Board were elected by Deputies and Senators by a 2/3 majority).

The management model outlined in the 1980 *Estatuto* was that of a public service strongly linked to the government and linked to political events in Spain (this is one of the principle criticisms made throughout the history of RTVE: Bustamante 2013).

Both in the era of the socialist governments of Felipe Gonzáles, and those of Aznar (who led the *Partido Popular Español* (PP) to form alliances with other political parties), no significant improvements were made to the mission or the organization of RTVE (the proposed reform of the RTVE statute collapsed in the face of any lack of agreement on the figure of the Director General and his appointment. The

PP wanted a stronger figure to be appointed by the government whereas the *Partido Socialista Obrero Español* (PSOE) opted for a more widely elected figure who had to secure a 2/3 majority in Parliament. Rather than strengthening PSB, the passage "from the era of public monopolies to the era of private oligopolies" (Tusell Gomez 2004) with the opening of the Spanish TV market to private initiative (*Ley* 31/1987 on Telecommunications and *Ley* 10/1988 on Private Television) initiated the recession of RTVE. With rising debts and a decrease in audience, the Spanish public broadcaster became one of the least successful in Europe.

Even in recent times, certain Spanish commentators have quite severely criticized the media, especially radio and television, stating that "just as occurs in some countries that are similar at a political and cultural level [the media] alternate between propaganda and advertising depending on whether they are publicly or privately owned. Namely, they swing between ideology and business" (González Ballestreros 2006, p. 13).

The twenty years of RTVE management by Directors-General linked in various ways to the government in office at the time confirms Spain's inclusion in Hallin and Mancini's Mediterranean model (Chapter 2).

Only later did *Ley* 17/2006 establish a change, entrusting the nomination of the Director-General (now the President), and of all members of the Board to the Congress of Deputies (Article 11).

Ley 17/2006 is the first radical reform of PSB to be attempted in the almost thirty years since the Constitution came into force. The structural changes are part of a larger framework of public broadcasting reform presented by the *Consejo para la reforma de los medios de comunicación de titularidad del Estado*, set up by the Zapatero Government (*Real Decreto* 744/2004) and made up of five "wise heads" who are communications experts.

The aim was that the governmental domination that had characterized RTVE should give way to greater independence from politics in line with modern radio and television services (for commentary on these changes, see Chinchilla Marín 2007).

The reform is based on a number of key points:

- the creation of *Corporación* RTVE as a public commercial company, independent of the government (Articles 3.1 and 5);
- Parliament's approval of framework agreements (*mandatos-marcos*) to establish the general objectives of the public broadcaster;

- the creation of some supervisory bodies for the public broadcaster and participation by civil society (*Consejos de Informativos* e *Consejo Asesor*);
- the election of the 12 members of the Board by the Parliament (8 proposed by the *Congreso*, of which 2 would be proposed by the trade unions "with greater representation at state level and represented in RTVE and its companies" and 4 by the *Senado*), by a 2/3 majority for a term of six years (Article 11); the President is elected by Parliament within the Board (Article 17).

The initial draft law provided for the appointment of the Director General by the Board, but in the final version, election by the *Congreso* was preferred.

The 2006 reform formally removed the government's power to appoint the President and the collegiate body, entrusting this role to Parliament.

The new system of appointments of the RTVE bodies should be considered within the context of Spanish parliamentary system, that favours the Executive, usually based on a strong majority.

However, the majoritarian conception of the electoral law, together with a parliamentary system dominated by the Executive, means that actually the power of appointment remains firmly in the hands of the Executive. The outcome that should arise from the application of the proportional electoral formula is, in fact, offset, on the one hand, by the division of electoral constituencies into very small colleges and, secondly, by the almost complete hegemony of the two major parties (PSOE and PP), that until recently, alternated in leading the country. As we know, this produces effects more similar to a majoritarian system than to a proportional one.

If we add to this, the fact that the choice of the President (and the RTVE Board members) elected and, possibly revoked, comes about with a 2/3 majority of the *Congreso* (Article 11, para. 4 *Ley* 17/2006) the effectiveness of this shift towards the "despolitización o independencia" from the government, as promoted by Zapatero government of the time, may appear questionable (Ortega Gutiérrez 2008, p. 229).

Formally, the nominations have been removed from the hands of the Executive, provided that the qualified majority leads to the involvement of minorities, but actually this power remains fully in the orbit of the political majority at any given time.

The reform of April 2012 confirmed this interpretation and has further weakened the (formal) guarantee introduced in 2006: with *Real Decreo-Ley* 15/2012 of 20 April, the Council of Ministers (PP) made some targeted changes to the appointments system described above, lowering the majority threshold and reducing the number of members on the Board.

The Decree provides that, "if within 24 hours of the first vote the 2/3 majority is not reached, the *Congreso de los Diputados* will appoint the President of *Corporación* RTVE and the Consejo by absolute majority." The government regained the *Disposición transitoria cuarta* of Law 17/2006 envisaged for the first mandate of the Board Members in order to tackle the problem of a possible failure to reach a 2/3 majority. The use of a decree law was justified by the government due to the extreme urgency needed to resolve the problem of the RTVE Presidency that had been empty since July 2011, leading to the risk of deadlock in the management of the public broadcaster (for instance, the President's powers included the preparation of the financial statements). Two Presidents had resigned without completing the mandate. The resignation of the first, Luis Fernández, was attributed to the clash with the government on the new financing system (*Ley* 8/2009 de *Financiación de la Corporación de Radio y Televisión Española*); while it would seem that the resignation of the latter, Albert Oliart, was related to nepotism (a contract awarded by RTVE to an enterprise whose sole director was the son of President Oliart himself). The position remained vacant due to the lack of agreement between the two major political parties on a competent and independent personality to appoint as President (Linde Paniagua 2013, p. 187).

To limit public expenditure, the number of Board members was reduced to 9 (5 elected by the Chamber of Deputies and 4 by the Senate); hence, the two members proposed by the most representative trade unions were removed and the Board once again became the full responsibility of the Parliament (or rather of the parliamentary majority, since the 24-hour limit applied also to this election).

Many have interpreted this measure as yet another example of the conflict between the PP and the PSOE, that in this case spills over into public service broadcasting, while some scholars considered it to be incompatibile with European Union Law (Linde Paniagua 2013).

The controversy has moved on to the figure of the new President of the Board, Leopoldo Gonzáles-Echenique, a former state attorney accused by the press of having removed many broadcasting executives and professionals from their posts: "What happened in the former public body is what always happens: the government changes and the wave expands to generate a tsunami that destroys everything" (Gómez Rosario 2012). In January 2012, after Mariano Rajoy took office (PP), a group of academics, scholars and communication professionals published *Teletodos, Manifiesto en Defensa of the Servicio Público Audiovisual.*

A return to the past has recently taken place with *Ley* 5/2017 of 29 September, which modifies *Ley* 17/2006, emblematically entitled: "*de la radio y televisión de titularidad estatal, para recuperar la indipendencia de la Corporación RTVE y el pluralismo en la elección parlamentaria de sus órganos.*" The law affects the composition and appointment of the 10 members of the Board. They will be elected by Parliament by a two-thirds majority: 6 by the Congress and 4 by the Senate, for a six-year non-renewable mandate. The new Article 11 stipulates that candidates must appear before the Congress and the Senate in a public hearing, in order for both Chambers to verify the suitability of the candidates for the office they are to occupy. The President of the RTVE *Corporación* and the Board will be elected by the Congress among the 10 members, by a majority of two-thirds, thus marking a return to the formula initially introduced by the Zapatero Government, though with a greater focus on the public selection process of the members.

France

France has always provided an example of the interference of politics (or more precisely the Executive) on public service broadcasting. It is no accident that this country's experience in broadcasting has become emblematic, giving rise to some of the terminology used by PSB scholars and the media in general (Chapter 2). What Humphreys defines as the "governative model" (Humphreys 1996) corresponds to the control of PSB by the Executive; a model that circulated widely in the early phase of the development of television systems and was common to many Countries (Hallin and Mancini 2004), but which in France took the form of political control over the entire broadcasting system ("politics over broadcasting" as it was classified by Kelly et al. 2002).

This approach, already visible in the original state monopoly of *Radiodiffusion et télévision de France* (RTF) during the Fourth Republic, was further strengthened with the passage from the parliamentary to the semi-presidential system.

In all the "three ages" of the French TV identified by the literature, although with different nuances and techniques for penetration, the strong presence of France's Presidents and of the governmental apparatus can be felt (Kuhn 2010).

In the early period (1956–1982), French TV "was integrated into an institutionalized system of political domination built around the Gaullist party" (Chevallier 1982, pp. 555–556). President de Gaulle almost immediately showed himself to be a formidable presence on the small screen, or the "*homme du petit écran*" (as defined by Brizzi 2014). Later de Gaulle built an organic relationship with the medium of television: "Le Président fait corp avec l'instrument, comme celui-ci, plus tard, ne fera qu'un avec le parti gaulliste. La télévision, prolongement d'un homme et d'un myte" (Blum 1984, p. 30).

The brutal and only faintly masked tools used under his presidency were then followed by the (softer) mechanism of the appointment of professionals "close" to the ruling political power (the so-called "professionalization of political control.") *Loi* n. 64-621 abolished RTF and set up the *Office de radio-télévision française* (ORTF) that was no longer directly controlled, but rather under the *tutelle* of the Minister of Information. The relationship between state and television underwent a change in 1969, with the introduction of the so-called "three-thirds rule," which laid down the amount of time allocated to minority parties in the television debate (one third to the government, one third to the parliamentary majority, one third to the opposition). Within the same period of reform *Loi* n. 74-469 effected the dissolution of ORTF and entrusted the public broadcasting service to seven public bodies.

The second "era" commenced with the *Loi organique* n. 82-652 which put an end to the state monopoly and lasted until the end of the 1990s. In those years, direct contact with the political sphere relaxed slightly thanks to the institution of the *Haute Autorité de la Communication audiovisuelle*, an independent Authority that took over responsibility for appointments. For the first time the Directors (or more precisely, the Presidents) of the public service broadcaster were not selected by the government. However, the High Authority comprised nine members appointed—three each—by the President of the Republic, the President of the National Assembly and the President of the Senate.

The lack of independence of these institutions meant that the problem of politicization was not entirely resolved.

The last period (from the mid-90s to the present day), is still characterized by the strong role played by politics, despite the establishment of the *Conseil Supérieur de l'Audiovisuel* (CSA), the body which now supervises and controls broadcasting and is involved in the appointment of the members of the Board of *France Télévisions* (in order to counteract the excessive power of political appointees).

The Sarkozy Presidency opened with the appointment of a *Commission pour la nouvelle télévision publique*, chaired by Jean-François Copé; the report published on 25 June 2008 was used to present two draft laws that were approved the following year. The 2009 reform[9] states the President's intention to actively participate in the appointment of the top figures in the national companies, thus relegating the CSA to a purely advisory role, and to autonomously take fundamental decisions for the survival of the public broadcaster.[10]

The power of appointment thus shifted to the French President for a period equal to the presidential term (five years), after consultation with the CSA and subject to the consent of the parliamentary committees, required to express their consent with a 3/5 majority. These guarantees should be considered in the light of the way the semi-presidential system functions in France, especially following the reform aimed at reducing the risk of cohabitation and thus the President's ability to count on a solid majority in parliament during his tenure.

If we consider that in addition to this presidential power, the government and the parliamentary committees nominate most of the board members (8 out of 14 plus the President), this leads to a domination by

[9]There were two laws: *Loi* n. 2009-257 on audiovisual communication and the public service and *Loi* 2009-258, as well as on the appointment of the Presidents of France Télévisions, Radio France and the company responsible for overseas broadcasting, both passed the scrutiny of the *Conseil constitutionnel* (DC N. 2009-576 e DC N. 2009-577).

[10]Such as the statement to eliminate advertising from television channels made during the press conference of January 2008, when Sarkozy surprised everyone including the relevant Minister and the President of France Télévisions, who apparently learned the news live at the press conference (Chapter 5). According to commentators, Sarkozy, in proposing a model in line with the BBC, free from the "tyranny of advertising," made a 'shrewdly calculated political choice', given the aversion of the opposition parties, particularly the Socialist Party, to the public service broadcaster's dependence on commercial advertising (Kuhn 2010, p. 7).

the government or, more generally, of the "government majority" that we could define as "institutionalized" (in the semi-presidential form of government).[11]

In fact, some commentators have labelled the intervention of the parliamentary committees as "window dressing in a futile attempt to mask a dramatic increase in direct presidential control of FTV" (Levy 2010, p. 8). There is no need to underscore the importance of the appointment of the President of FTV who, among other things, enjoys an important role in the choice of the organization's top management body; many scholars agree on the lack of effectiveness of the reforms and the danger of a return to the years of strong ties between politics and television (Regourd 2009, pp. 29–34; Rambaud and Roblot-Troizier 2009, pp. 585–588; Verpeaux 2009, pp. 15–18).

Following the reform, *Le Nouvel Observateur* in its "édition de jeudi" (11 December 2008) published an open letter from workers in the audiovisual sector asking Sarkozy to "amender profondément" the text, "pour en corriger les vices et les excès." The reform was indeed regressive, a return to the period of ORTF when the Directors of the PSB were appointed directly by the government.

At a more substantive level, the government's influence is evident through its approval of the *Estatuts* of *France Télévisions* and other broadcasting companies, as well as the *cahiers des charges*, i.e. the documents that define the public service mission covering key issues such as the PSB's educational, cultural and social programmes, and the obligations on communication in specific times that are critical for national defense, public safety and government communication in times of crisis.

Loi n. 2013-1028 of 15 November 2013 concerning the *indépendance de l'audiovisuel public* has changed the system of appointments explained above, so that now the President of *France Télévisions* (and *France Radio*) is chosen by the CSA, which in turn was the subject of new regulations on appointments (the new CSA consists of

[11]This can be inferred from, for example, the so-called *right to air time* and the *right to replay*, that are compulsory for PSBs. The party system (and the inevitable impact on the form of government) is characterized by a strong separation between the majority and the opposition; this also impacts the way in which air time is allocated, whereby the Parliamentary groups are favoured (clearly divided between the majority and the opposition), to the detriment of small minority groups. For this reason the CSA intervened by issuing a set of rules to facilitate access even to non-represented groups, acting as a guarantor of political pluralism.

7 members, including the President, who is appointed by the President of the French Republic; 3 members are appointed by the President of the National Assembly and 3 by the President of the Senate) and the 14 board members of *France Télévisions* are allocated as follows: 2 MPs (chosen by the Culture Commission of the National Assembly and the Senate); 5 representatives of the State; 5 independent persons appointed by the CSA; 2 members appointed in compliance with Loi n. 83-675 of 26 July 1983 concerning the *démocratisation du secteur public* representing the employees of France TV.

The CSA reform thus has a cascade effect on the composition of the top posts of the PSB; the power of the President of the Republic is limited in order to promote wider participation and fragmentation in the appointments.

Conclusion

An analysis of some European experiences, selected according to the way the public broadcasters' managing bodies are appointed (from formally parliamentary to substantially governmental), leads us to reflect on where the power to appoint really lies and whether parliamentary appointment is a real guarantee of the independence of PSB.

A closer examination of the normative data collected enables us to state that the initial trend noted in the prevalence of Parliaments in the selection of the members managing PSB should be reconsidered to take account of the form of government operating in a country, as well as its electoral and party system.

This does not mean that there is a direct link (cause and effect) between forms of government and the incidence of political power on the public broadcaster. Thus, it does not follow that a form of government "dominated by the Executive" will correspond to governmental powers as appointee (theoretically detrimental to the independence of PSB), while the "dominance of Parliament" will necessarily correspond to a greater power of appointment by parliament with decisions taken within the Chamber (and, therefore, offering greater guarantee of independence).

Rather one should reason on the link between the information system and the form of government; where information—understood as freedom but also as power—reflects and determines the form of government (in turn influenced by the electoral system), especially in countries where the media play a fundamental role during election campaigns and may determine the results of elections. Here, more than anywhere else, the role of the public broadcasting service as the guarantor of information emerges.

This analysis allows us to better understand the appointments mechanism and to thus disavow the apparent initial trend towards a prevalence of Parliament in the selection of the Board members of the public broadcasters, highlighting the constant presence of governmental interference.

In Spain, the 2006 reform formally removed the power to appoint the Director-General and the Board from the government and entrusted it to Parliament, but the "majoritarian trend" of the electoral law, together with a parliamentary system in which the government predominates, means that the authority to appoint essentially remains firmly in the hands of the group in government. The reform of April 2012 confirmed this interpretation.

In France, much of the Board of *France Télévision* (as well as the President) is practically government-appointed, despite the involvement of the parliamentary committees (that must express a 3/5majority) and the *Conseil Supérieur de l'Audiovisuel.*

In the United Kingdom (where, historically, the Labour and the Conservative Parties alternated in leading the country), the monarch formally made all appointments until the time of the new Royal Charter, though they were, in fact, nominated by the government.

In Italy, until the political and judicial upsets of the 1990s, the political system was characterized by a strong multi-partyism, with some parties dominating over the others; this led to the phenomenon of "parcelling-out" mentioned earlier. Only for a brief period, with the introduction of the majoritarian electoral system and some adjustments (coalition bonus, minimum threshold, etc.) was it possible to identify a clear (coalition) majority. This parliamentary majority was represented proportionally in the RAI Supervisory Committee, thus influencing the choice of the members of the Board of the Italian public broadcaster.

The political scenario has changed profoundly over the last few years, or rather the last rounds of elections have failed to produce clear victories for the historical parties (or coalitions). A number of factors have contributed to this outcome (the economic crisis, the crisis of institutional political parties, the success of new cultural and political movements: the Five-Star Movement and Podemos, as well as the Brexit Referendum among others). This has had important consequences at the institutional level: in Spain, the failure of the *Partido Popular* to achieve a majority in the December 2015 and June 2016 elections led to an interim Government headed by Mariano Rajoy for almost a year; in the United Kingdom, the early elections of June 2017 called by the incumbent Prime Minister Theresa May, led to a hung parliament; in Italy, the approval of the new electoral law (Law 165/2017) was lengthy and tortuous and was accompanied by a Constitutional Court ruling that declared an important part of the previous electoral law to be unconstitutional (judgment 35/2017 relating to Law 52/2015); in the span of one legislature, three different governments have succeeded each other.

References

Barendt, E. (1994). Legal aspects of BBC Charter renewal. *Political Quarterly, 65*, 20–28.

Barnett, S. (2005). Opportunity or threat? The BBC, investigative journalism and the Hutton report. In S. Allan (Ed.), *Journalism: Critical issues*. London: Open University Press.

BBC. (2004). *Building public value: Renewing the BBC for a digital world*. London: Duke University Press.

BBC. (2013, December). *Review of BBC internal governance. A joint review by the BBC trust and the BBC Executive Board*. http://downloads.bbc.co.uk/bbctrust/assets/files/pdf/about/how_we_govern/governance_review_2013.pdf.

Blum, S. (1984). La télévision ordinaire du pouvoir. *Réseaux, 2*(9), 23–57.

Brizzi R. (2014). *De Gaulle et les médias. L'homme du petit écran*. Rennes: Presses universitaires de Rennes.

Bustamante, E. (2013). *Historia de la radio y la televisión en España. Una asignatura pendiente de la democracia*. Barcelona: Gedisa.

Chevallier, J. (1982). Le statut de la communication audiovisuelle. *Actualité juridique Droit Administratif*, 555–576.

Chinchilla Marín, C. (2007). La reforma de la radio y la televisión publicas de titularidad estatal: la Ley 17/2006, de 5 de junio. *Revista de Administración Pública, 174*(1), 293–333.

Donders, K., & Pauwels, C. (2010). The introduction of an ex ante evaluation for new media services: Is Europe asking for it, or does public service broadcasting need it? *International Journal of Media & Cultural Politics, 6*(2), 133–148.

Freedman, D. (2016). Decoding the BBC white paper. *The Future of BBC*. https://www.opendemocracy.net/ourbeeb/des-freedman/decoding-BBC-white-paper.

Frosini, T. E. (2015). *Liberté, Egalité, Internet*. Napoli: Editoriale scientifica.

Gardini, G. (2007). Broagcasting, the free market and the public interest: Is the Italian path to pluralism viable? *European Public Law, 13*(2), 239–261.

Gardini, G. (2008). Dal «servizio pubblico» al «sistema» radiotelevisivo: la breve storia di un grande fallimento. *Diritto pubblico*, 637–674.

Gómez Rosario, G. (2012). *La contrarreforma de Rtve*. El País 4 agosto.

González Ballestreros, T. (2006). Mezzi di comunicazione e sviluppo democratico in Spagna. In G. Guidi (Ed.), *La società dell'informazione: libertà, pluralismo, riforme. Atti del convegno di San Marino, 30 settembre 2005*. Torino: Giappichelli.

Hallin, D. C., & Mancini, P. (2004). *Comparing media systems: Three models of media and politics*. New York: Cambridge University Press.

Humphreys, P. (1996). *Mass media and media policy in Western Europe*. Manchester: Manchester University Press.

Jakubowicz, K. (2007). Public service broadcasting in 21st century: What chance for a new beginning? In G. Ferrel Lowe & J. Bardoel (Eds.), *From public service broadcasting to public service media*. Gothenburg: Nordicom.

Katsirea, I. (2008). *Public broadcasting and European Law. A comparative examination of public service obligations in six member states*. Austin: Kluwer Law International.

Kelly, G., Muers, S., & Mulgan, G. (2002). *Creating public value: An analytical framework for public service reform*. London: Cabinet Office Strategy Unit.

Kuhn, R. (2010). *Public service television in Sarkozy's France*, Paper presented at the Conference RIPE@2010: Public Service Media after the recession, available on RIPE website.

Levy, D. (2010). *PSB policymaking in comparative perspective: The BBC Charter review process and the French Commission pour la nouvelle télévision publique*, Paper presented at the Conference RIPE@2010: Public Service Media after the recession, available on RIPE website.

Linde Paniagua, E. (2013). Las mutaciones del régimen jurídico de la televisión pública estatal y su incompatibilidad con el derecho de la Unión Europea. *Revista de Derecho de la Unión Europea, 24*(enero-junio), 183–200.

Munro, C. (1979). *Television, censorship and the law*. London: Saxon House.

Moe, H. (2010). Governing public service broadcasting: 'Public value tests' in different national contexts. *Communication, Culture & Critique, 3*, 207–223.

Moore, M. (1995). *Creating public value: Strategic management in government*. Cambridge: Harvard University Press.

Morgan, J. (1986). The BBC and the concept of public service broadcasting. In C. McCabe & O. Stewart (Eds.), *The BBC and public service broadcasting*. Manchester: Manchester University Press.

Muñoz Saldaña, M. (2008). The future of public service broadcasting in Community law. *International Journal of Media & Cultural Politics, 4*(2), 203–219.

Ortega Gutiérrez, D. (2008). *El derecho a la comunicación. Un análisis juridico-periodístico*. Madrid: Centro de Estudios Ramón Areces.

Pavani, G. (2017, August). Anomalies of the Italian public service broadcasting despite the law 220 of 2015. *European Public Law*, *23*(3), 507–524.

Prosser, T. (2007). *United Kingdom, in Iris special. The public service broadcasting culture*. Strasbourg: European Audiovisual Observatory.

Regourd, S. (2009). La loi du 5 mars 2009 et le nouveau service public de la télévision: une régénération controversée. *Légipresse, 260*.

Rambaud, T., & Roblot-Troizier, A. (2009). Cronique de jurisprudence - Droit administratif et Droit constitutionnel. *Revue française de droit administratif, 3*, 580–596.

Tusell Gomez, J. (2004). *El Aznarato: el gobierno del partido popular, 1996–2003*. Madrid: Aguilar.

Verpeaux, M. (2009). Liberté de communication et pouvoir de nomination du président de la République. La Semaine juridique. *Édition générale,18*.

Zeno-Zencovich, V. (2010). *La nuova televisione europea. Commento al "Decreto Romani"*. Rimini: Maggioli Editore.

CHAPTER 7

Conclusions

Abstract This chapter is dedicated to the concluding considerations. After specifying that the study of broadcasting systems through the juxtaposition of the two historical models (US-commercial and European-public service) appears of limited use, and that the rigid legal taxonomy based on the legal nature of the broadcaster—and on the form of state as a meta-parameter—immediately appeared inadequate, the Author 'breaks up' the class of public service broadcasting into different elements that she considers crucial. Each of these elements may be used to test the extent to which the public broadcaster is effectively "public", and hence its adherence to its mission. These elements are: the degree of decentralization; the funding methods; internal organization and relations with political institutions.

Keywords US-commercial model · European model · Legal taxonomy Public service broadcasting · Decentralization · Funding methods

Public Service Broadcasting: Breaking Down the Model

In an era that has witnessed a revolution in the broadcasting scenario due to the introduction of new platforms, studying broadcasting systems through the juxtaposition of the two historical models (US-commercial and European-public service) appears of limited use. "All public service

G. Pavani, *The Structure and Governance of Public Service Broadcasting*, https://doi.org/10.1007/978-3-319-96731-8_7

media organizations now operate within a wider, potentially global, market, characterised by increasing competition and the disruptive power of new business models which are now competing directly for revenue with previously established players" (CM/Rec (2012) 1, N. I).

From the outset, the (few) attempts to classify the structure and organization of broadcasting systems showed limitations. The rigid taxonomy based on the legal nature of the broadcaster—and on the form of state as a meta-parameter—immediately appeared inadequate. The comparative analysis of circulation of these two models confirms the weakness of this approach. In fact, many of the countries frequently ascribed to a model based on the prestige or economic imposition of the dominant country present elements that are relevant to the alternative model. This was clearly evidenced in Chapter 2 in the discussion of the Latin-American experiences and their comparison with the US model.

Neither does the European model of Public service broadcasting stand as a monolith, despite the pressures at a supranational level for its uniformization (Chapter 3).

As far as the PSB mission is concerned, the European Union and the Council of Europe, though with different tools and purposes, have both adopted the inspiring principles of the British public service broadcaster, transforming them into principles shared by the member states (pluralism, independence from politics, cultural promotion, etc.). What I have defined as a prototype of PSB, has now risen like a phoenix from the cultural model of the BBC, "sifted" from the ashes by the supranational organizations and based on a series of pan-European standards, to survive in the new technological scenario of PSB 2.0 (Chapter 2).

This harmonizing influence also impacts on the structural and organizational side. A framework for the relationship between the mission and the organization of the public broadcaster has long been outlined by the CoE. In various documents, states are asked to rethink the governance of their public broadcasters to enable the shift from the role of state broadcaster—with strong links to the government, and weaker accountability to the wider audience or civil society—to that of an authentic public service media (CM/Rec (2012) 1, N. I). The CoE recommends that member states draw inspiration from the guiding principles of the Recommendation, thereby guaranteeing the independence and sustainable development of public service media.

The supranational level therefore tends to impose a single model (of efficient organization) on different cultural and political contexts. In fact, the states' public broadcasters have traditionally been organized differently, and often in an original way, thus reflecting differences in history and culture. The Recommendations on governance and the guidelines on how to best implement the common principles elaborated at supranational level become diluted in the face of state sovereignty, still expressed in the structure of the public broadcasters.

The study of the structural and organizational aspects of public broadcasters, therefore, serves to verify their substantial respect for their mission. This is possible through a comparative analysis that develops from the different state experiences, based on a careful assessment of the conditions of comparability and not, on the contrary, from a deductive inquiry into the standardizing criteria contained in the CoE's Recommendations.

The positive law analysis conducted in Chapter 5 provided a highly varied picture of the organizational solutions adopted for the European public broadcasters, which feature "many variables, few cases" (Lijphart 1971).

It has been observed that: "Reducing the number of variables by trapping them in sharply defined sets is not a suitable approach to studying social phenomena. [...] a suitable approach should be able to hold together in a logical and in a legal sense the largest number of items without losing the usefulness of the predictivity of the models" (Baldin 2017, p. 142).

Therefore, even a legal analysis may require us to hold together the greatest possible number of items and abandon the intensional classifications (that lead to rigid, monothetic categories) and adopt the extensional classifications (which provide polythetic categories), in which different items have something in common although no trait unites them all (for further information, see Marradi 1990, p. 130).

The use of rigid monothetic and, as such, antithetical categories is thus not recommended because it would be difficult to group such different experiences into a single class of governance of public broadcaster and would require a good degree of approximation.

To organize the data that emerged and maintain the many variables together it is necessary to "decompose" the class of public service broadcasting into different elements that I consider crucial. Each of these elements may be used to test to what extent the public broadcaster is effectively "public," and hence its adherence to the mission. These elements are: the degree of decentralization; the funding methods; internal organization and relations with political institutions. These act as parameters for sub-classes drawn up with the help of other social sciences and their predictive models in a prescriptive view, to make the analysis more faithful to the law in action.

The reassembling of the public service broadcasting class gives rise to a category with fuzzy outlines, in which the public broadcasters are placed along an axis according to the extent to which they belong, as deduced from the determining elements. At the centre we find the prototype PSB provided by the European institutions; the position of the public broadcasters along the axis would depend on the varying intensity of their public nature and their fulfillment of the typical mission of a public broadcasting service. This permits us to note certain features that would normally be overlooked in any analysis that aimed to group the public broadcasters in rigid classes (Pavani 2012, p. 278*ff*).

As regards structure, various forms of organization would be admitted in the PSB class: not only public bodies, but commercial companies, business associations and foundations, which perform a public function and are characterized by a high degree of independence (as in the Dutch or Swedish cases).

The level to which the single public broadcasting experiences are "public" is obtained through an assessment that combines the three elements listed below.

1. *The degree of decentralization*

This element indicates the respect of certain values typical of a public service, such as the promotion of local culture, the protection of ethnic and linguistic minorities and, more generally, regional identities.

The regional TV are subject to the internal dynamics and the centrifugal or centripetal thrusts that characterize the territorial form of the state (centralized or decentralized). However, classifications based exclusively on normative parameters linked to the territorial form of the state prove insufficient to test the real degree of decentralization of PSB. To appreciate the actual degree of "proximity" of a PSB to a territorial collectivity, further criteria were used such as television "production," or a combination of legal and extra-legal parameters (Chapter 5).

While in some federal states there is a correspondence between the form of state and the decentralization of the PSB because the establishment of the PSB and the federative process have developed in parallel (as in Germany, where the televisions belong to the Länder), or the federative structure of the state is characterized by strong linguistic identities and the PSB contribute to the implementation of cultural functions that belong to the respective Communities (as in Belgium), this is not always the case (for example, Austria).

This parallelism is not always achieved in regional states: the Italian experience of centralization places the RAI far from the centre of the axis (close to certain unitary states, such as Greece). Closer to the centre, we find Spain (whose position is determined by a balance between the centralized organization of RTVE, which would place the country close to Italy, and the experiences of regional TV broadcasters that, however, push it closer to the federal states) and the United Kingdom (where the BBC's Nations and Regions Division has been reorganized and most of the production activities have been reorganized in local offices).

The public broadcasters of states which, legally, from the viewpoint of the distribution of legislative powers, are considered centralized (e.g. Denmark and the Netherlands) or weakly decentralized (e.g. Portugal), are sometimes structured to better represent and protect the values of local communities than the public broadcasters of the regional states. Elements such as the differentiation of television production in accordance with the specific characteristics of the territory and the composition of the body that determines the programming policies of the broadcaster (representative of the main cultural, religious, and worker movements) lead to place the Danish TV2 and the Dutch provincial TV broadcasters among the group of countries with a good degree of broadcasting decentralization.

2. *Funding*

The position on the axis based on this component, is determined not only by the type of funding chosen, but also by *how* it is determined, and the way the funding collected from users is spent.

Excessive use of sources of a commercial nature (especially advertising) tends to weaken the public nature of the radio and television service and leads to a greater distancing from the centre of the axis, especially when the ratio between the public funding source (be it the licence fee or another subsidy) and the private source, is equal (as it was until recently in Italy and Ireland). The countries that have opted for funding derived from the state budget, including Belgium, the Netherlands, Latvia and Lithuania, maintain a good balance. Funding derived only from the licence fee is considered appropriate to the public mission and attests a high degree of independence of PSB, as evidenced by the historical cases of the United Kingdom and the Scandinavian countries (there is some doubt about the recent French reform, partly because of the difficulties involved in its implementation). The revenues derived from the licence fee are almost always supplemented by income from commercial activities of various kinds that, however, account for a low proportion of the total funding. The same reasoning applies to public state financing as the sole source of funding; for some years there has been a tendency to abandon the licence fee (e.g. Finland) and advertising (e.g. Spain) in favour of varying forms of subsidies from the either state or local authorities, depending on which is responsible. Often this choice fits into a framework of overall renewal of the public broadcaster (the Spanish experience of RTVE mentioned above is emblematic).

In addition to the type, the manner by which the funding is determined is also important to establish each country's position on the axis. The choice of the body called upon to approve the amount of public funding (licence fee or subsidy) may affect the degree to which the public broadcaster is "public." In many countries this task falls to the government (or more specifically, to the Minister responsible for Communications); in others to the Parliament (as in the Scandinavian countries and in Switzerland). Only very rarely does an independent authority intervene (as in Germany and Ireland). The level of funding and its duration are also important.

In the case of fee-based funding, it is also necessary to assess whether the whole amount collected is used to fund the public broadcaster; it is reinvested (e.g. in Belgium, the financial subsidies given by the French community government to RTBF.Be come from the licence fee paid by the residents) or, as in decentralized states, it is shared out equally (e.g. in Switzerland, the licence fee is the same for all the subscribers of all Cantons, making it possible to satisfy the mandate granted by the Federal Council to the public broadcaster: to produce and transmit a certain number of programmes throughout the territory in the four languages).

3. *Internal organization and relationship with political institutions*

The legal approach to the study of the internal organization of the public broadcasters is usually limited to the description of how the members of the management bodies are appointed, the duration of tenure and any conflict of interests. Usually, the legal categories used to test the degree of independence of some public subjects/bodies and/or administrative authorities are almost automatically applied to the public broadcasters without adaptation. Hence, no recognition is given to the fact that PSB is an institution at the service of a fundamental freedom that has always been closely connected with the political expression of a country (the public broadcasting service acts a spokesperson for political persuasions while at the same time being partly, and inevitably, influenced by them).

The relationship between the public broadcasters and the political institutions is "something that" goes beyond the normative data and resists insertion in the legal taxonomies held by the jurist. It is a "historical, political and cultural" factor that will deeply characterize a country and may at the same time, unite it to other countries that are apparently different.

The analysis of the appointment systems of the top organs of broadcasters provides partial results, that may be misleading and fail to explain how similar rules lead to different results or why no interference occurs even where the existing regulations would permit extensive government interference, as in the much-cited case of the British experience.

As has been noted, applying Lijphart's theses to communication systems, "often identical legislative norms produce different effects in majority and consensual systems" (Hallin and Mancini 2004, p. 48), and this is what sometimes happens with parliamentary appointment of Board members.

The empirical analysis carried out in Chapter 6 made it possible to interpret the normative data through the lens of the form of government adopted and evolved over time, in a different way in the four emblematic Countries, thus providing a key to a more faithful reading of the law in action.

Nonetheless, this intangible link between the media and the political institutions reveals the intrinsic characteristics of certain media, especially PSB. This "element" that can only be understood from the perspective of an overall analysis that considers both the recorded and non-recorded norms, those that complement the legal order and that "people practice without being fully aware of it" (Sacco 2015).

It is, therefore, necessary to integrate the analysis with tools developed by other sciences, which investigate the relationship and the reciprocal influences between media and politics. We have to contextualize the legal data in "empirical, non-normative" models, starting from the general ones on the media (the three models of journalistic information proposed by Hallin and Mancini that frame different cultural contexts) and advancing to those on broadcasting systems and on public broadcasters in particular (Humphreys' four models of public media governance compared to the various forms of control by political forces), mentioned to in Chapter 2.

Furthermore, even the CoE realized that "the detail of appointment procedures, the terms of tenure and permissible grounds for dismissal, conflicts of interest and methods by which the organisation will be held accountable [...] are all of fundamental importance in a proper and well-functioning governance system, [but] they must be placed in a broader context (CM/Rec (2012) 1, N. I).

The contextualization of the three countries examined in the Mediterranean model (Italy, Spain, France), provides some answers to the various attempts to explain the actual functioning of the internal organization of the public broadcasters, the appointments of Board members and the control systems, and stimulates some reflections on what we initially called a "historical-political-cultural" factor and now, with the support of the studies just mentioned, is revealed as a particularly invasive cultural formant that profoundly influences the legal systems within this class. This formant integrates the positive law and should enable us to understand the context in which the media operate and hence propose (normative) solutions suited to the cultural characteristics of a country. As scholars have noted, "the need to evaluate the "cryptotypes" and the dissociation between formants in no way means that the positivist approach to comparison should be abandoned, rather it emphasizes the issues raised, obviously not only by the law, and enhances law in action, to draw elements of understanding and then of comparison from it" (Pegoraro and Rinella 2013, p. 42). Moreover, it increasingly requires the aid of tools and methods created and implemented by other sciences.

The changes currently occurring in some countries belonging to the Mediterranean model could be interpreted in this perspective of dissociation of formants: some governments are responding to the cultural problems of their broadcasting services by performing "legal microsurgery" on the regulations, preferring to adjust the internal organization of the broadcaster rather than attempt a comprehensive redesign of PSB that has long been in crisis in these countries.

As in Spain, for example, where for a decade the main historical political parties, PP and PSOE, shuffle around the majorities required for the appointment of RTVE Board members: the 2006 reform attempted to remedy the politicization of RTVE, but the Decree of 20 April 2012 returned the country to its initial position, confirming the permanence of a political (or rather, governmental) influence on the composition of the broadcaster's top management bodies. The recent reform of 2017 has attempted to overturn this regression.

In France and Greece, for example, there is a new tendency to over-regulate the phases of election for the members of the managing bodies of public broadcasters, using traditional tools such as the aggravation of procedures, the greater involvement of independent bodies and authorities, in an attempt to loosen the link between politics and the media. France, by rewriting the rules on PSB governance, has "loosened" the power of presidential nomination and has "tightened" that of the *Conseil Supérieur de l'Audiovisuel* (whose members are now appointed by the Presidents of the two Houses). Instead, Greece has innovated the whole structure of the Board of the new public broadcaster, making the appointment procedures more transparent thanks to the establishment of a Supervisory Board, namely a guarantor placed between the public broadcaster and the political bodies.

It seems that the legislators of the two countries are trying to dominate the cultural factor discussed earlier (the link between media and politics), by "trapping" it within normative boarders. Such an approach is not in itself necessarily negative; indeed, we find different expressions of the same approach, even in countries whose public broadcasters are not really considered politicized. In the countries belonging to the corporate model, political parties are involved in the appointment of members of the managing bodies in the same way as other institutional subjects (trade unions, religious confessions, etc.). However, the studies of communication sciences indicate that it is difficult to change a context that feeds on history, traditions and local culture by making a few specific normative adjustments. In Italy, the "light" 2015 reform of the RAI which foresees a (potential) strengthening of some managerial figures, in theory seems not unrelated to solutions present in the comparatistic landscape.

However, if this reform is contextualized in a model that presents certain characteristics, it appears to contrast with the choices made in other countries that aim at removing the power of appointment from the government (by requiring a series of passages through connecting rings).

Concluding Reflections

A synthesis of these elements makes it possible to assign a rating to the various PSB, positioning them on the axis and moving them back and forth as if they were pawns, according to the most relevant changes.

However, if we were to consider only the normative analysis—even if integrated by the interpretation of data in the light of the functioning of the forms of government—the countries would be positioned on the axis according to the degree of "interference" by governmental appointment. Thus, we would find Italy, France and Spain (but formally also the United Kingdom!) on one edge of the axis, and the Scandinavian countries, the Netherland and Germany (to mention just the most relevant cases) on the opposite edge. In the first group of public broadcasters, the political influence on the choice of the members of the Boards and executive bodies—President or General Director—remains strong. Among the public services located towards the positive end of the axis are those that provide for the participation of employees in the Boards (e.g. Denmark, Ireland, Norway and Finland, even if in the latter case they are non-voting members) and those who have opened to civil society (Germany and the Netherlands).

The position on the axis can be modified—in a negative sense—as demonstrated by the cases of Hungary (the 2011 reform has, in fact, nullified much of the independence and pluralism that the media had won over the years) and Poland (2016 reform of PSM put public broadcasting under the direct control of the government and restricted the constitutional role of the existing media regulator, the National Media Council, in particular with regard to the composition and the selection mechanism of its members).

On the other hand, if we consider the cultural contexts in which the public broadcasters operate using the models of communications science mentioned above, then the individual countries would no longer move freely on the axis, but within their cultural context. In this context we could appreciate similarities and differences that might either move the countries nearer to the model or distance them from it.

In this sense, the (cultural) models would become prescriptive for supranational institutions that continue to advocate a standard of independence and pluralism of PSB without taking the historical-political-cultural characteristics of the state public broadcasters into account.

The renewed model of public service broadcasting has proved to be prescriptive especially for the countries of Eastern Europe, while sometimes the countries that have contributed to establishing the common principles fail to fully respect them (e.g. Italy, repeatedly called to respect the principle of independence of the media). Its validity is reinforced by its circulation beyond the European borders, in many countries that had already accepted the prototype PSB and have now confirmed it with legislative changes adapted to the new international standards. The same analysis scheme applied in greater depth to European countries may also be used for those outside Europe, where the PSB has developed along European lines. It can also be extended to other public broadcasters, even those created in typically commercial broadcasting systems. Nothing prevents us from using these tools to verify the degree of "publicness" of the American, Australian and New Zealand public broadcasters, and others besides, a publicness that is paradoxically high in the very countries characterized by commercial TV.

References

Baldin, S. (2017). Classifications and fuzzy logic: A comparative law perspective. In S. Bagni, G. Pavani, & G. Figueroa Mejía (Eds.), *La ciencia del derecho Constitucional comparado. Libro homenaje a Lucio Pegoraro Tomo I*. México: Editorial Tirant Lo Blanch.

Hallin, D. C., & Mancini, P. (2004). *Comparing media systems: Three models of media and politics*. New York: Cambridge University Press.

Lijphart, A. (1971). Comparative politics and the comparative method. *American Political Science Review, 65*, 682–693.

Marradi, A. (1990). Classification, typology, taxonomy. *Quality & Quantity, 24*, 129–157.

Pavani, G. (2012). *Radiotelevisioni. Profili storici e comparati*. Bologna: Filodiritto Editore.

Pegoraro, L., & Rinella, A. (2013). *Diritto costituzionale comparato. Aspetti metodologici*. Padova: CEDAM.

Sacco, R. (2015). *II diritto muto: Neuroscienze, conoscenza tacita, valori condivisi*. Bologna: il Mulino.

The manufacturer's authorised representative in the EU is Springer Nature Customer Service Centre GmbH, Europaplatz 3, 69115 Heidelberg, Germany. If you have any concerns regarding our products, please contact ProductSafety@springernature.com

Printed and bound by CPI Group (UK) Ltd, Croydon, CR0 4YY
30/09/2026
02225609-0016